LEVELS
of
INSANITY

A Ballantine Book
Published by The Random House Publishing Group

Some of the material has been previously published.

Ballantine and colophon are registered trademarks of Random House, Inc.

www.ballantinebooks.com

Library of Congress Control Number: 2004094174

ISBN 0-345-45095-7

Manufactured in the United States of America

1 3 5 7 9 8 6 4 2

First Edition: September 2004

Book design by Susan Turner

LEVELS
of
INSANITY

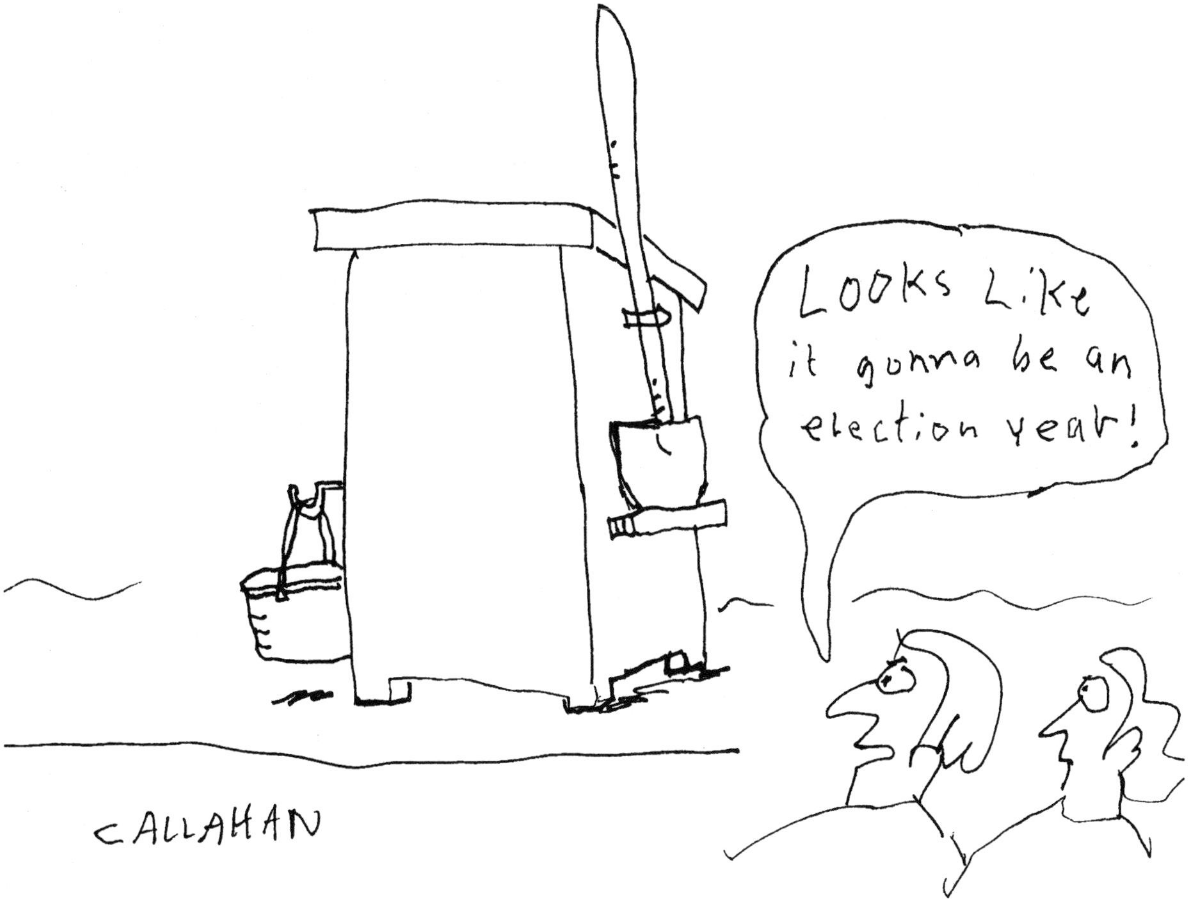
LOOKS LIKE it gonna be an election year!
CALLAHAN

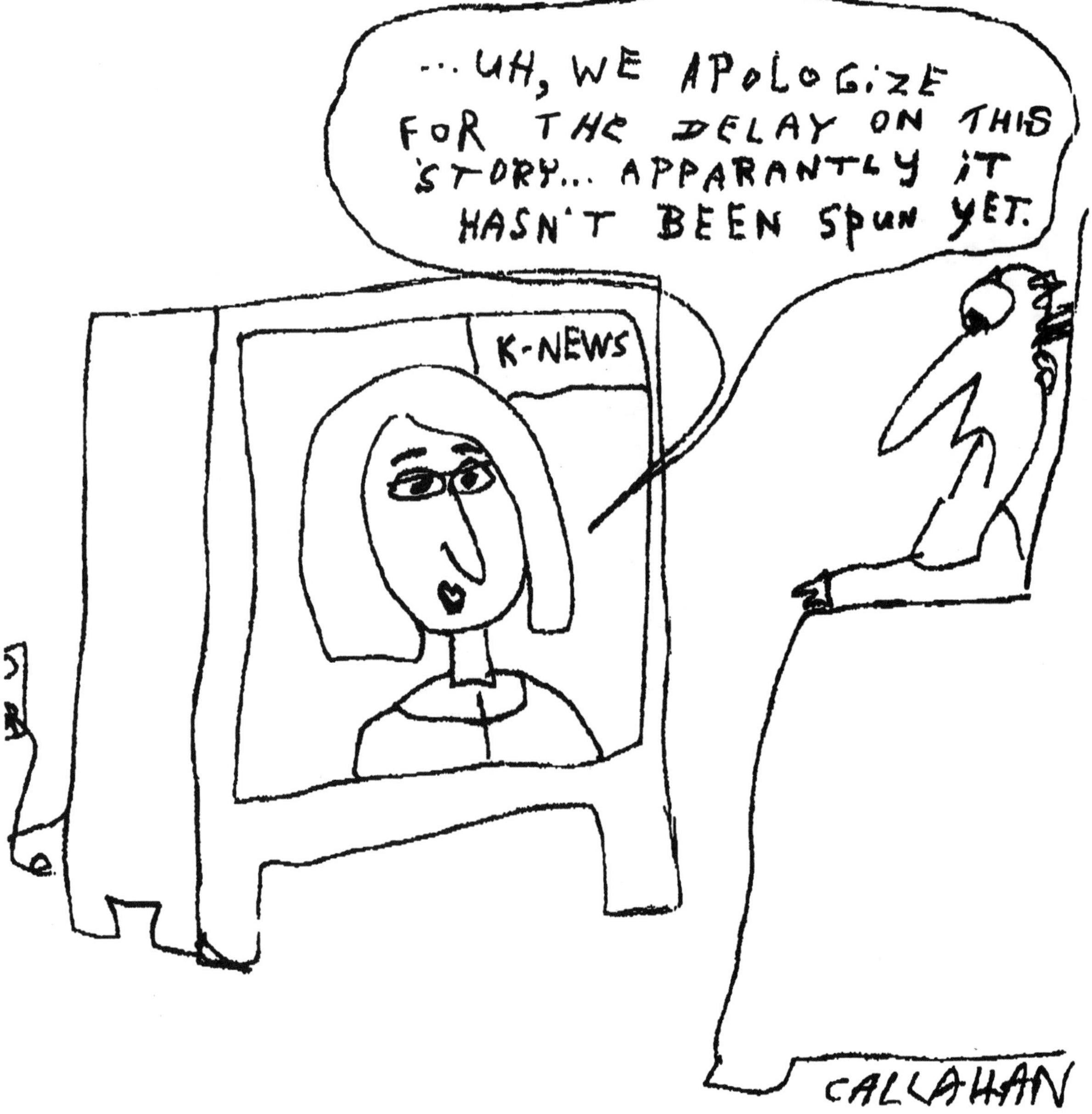
...UH, WE APOLOGIZE FOR THE DELAY ON THIS STORY... APPARANTLY IT HASN'T BEEN SPUN YET.
K-NEWS
CALLAHAN

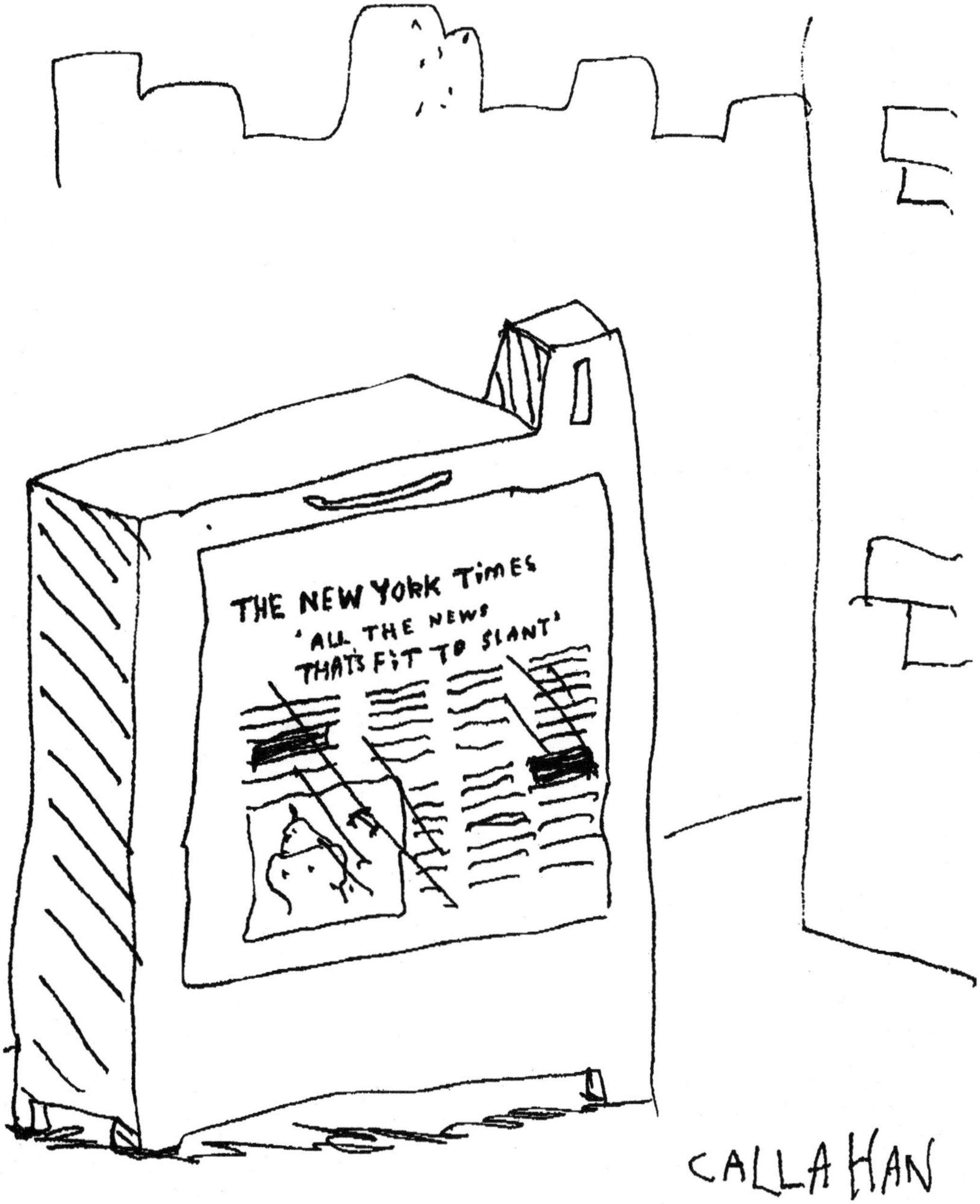
THE NEW YORK TIMES
'ALL THE NEWS
THAT'S FIT TO SLANT'
CALLAHAN

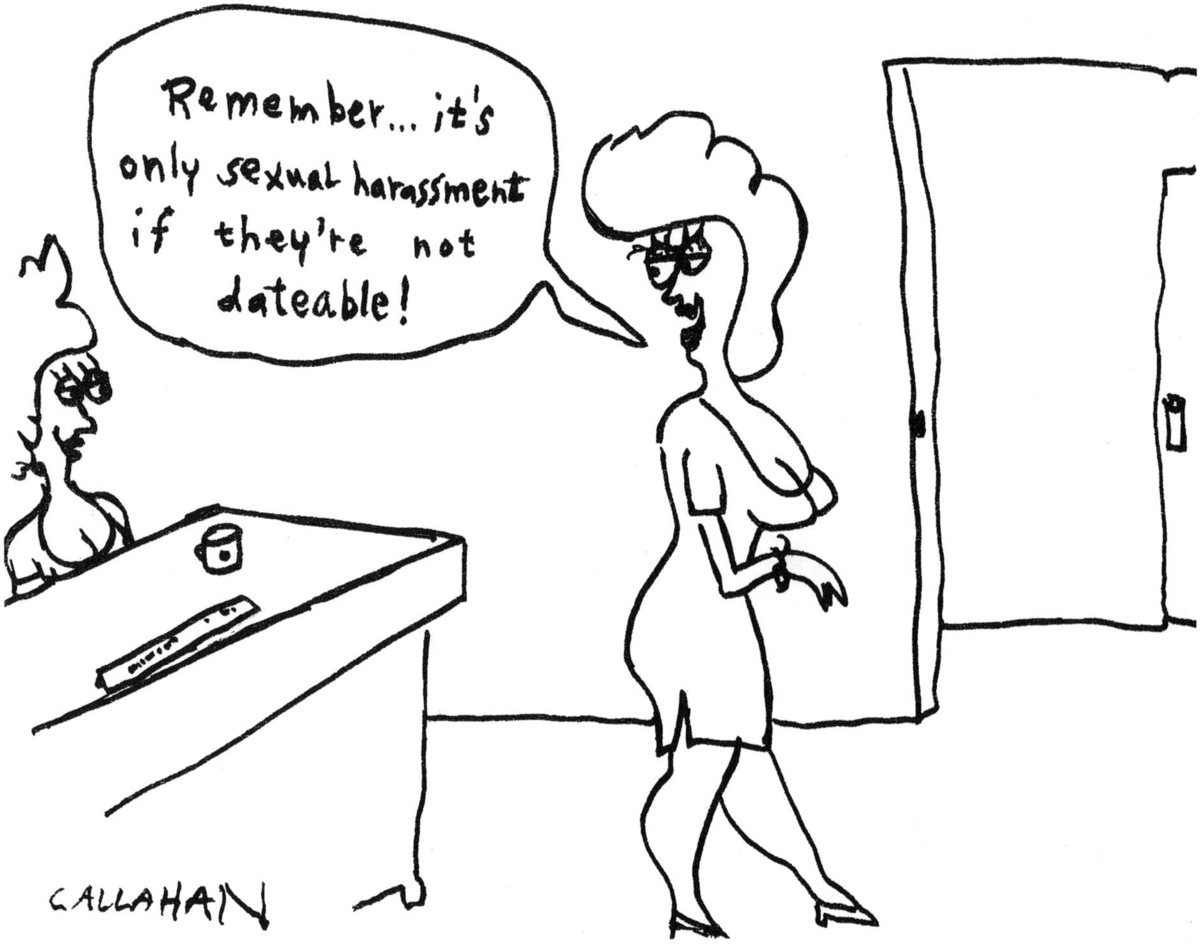
Remember... it's only sexual harassment if they're not dateable!
CALLAHAN

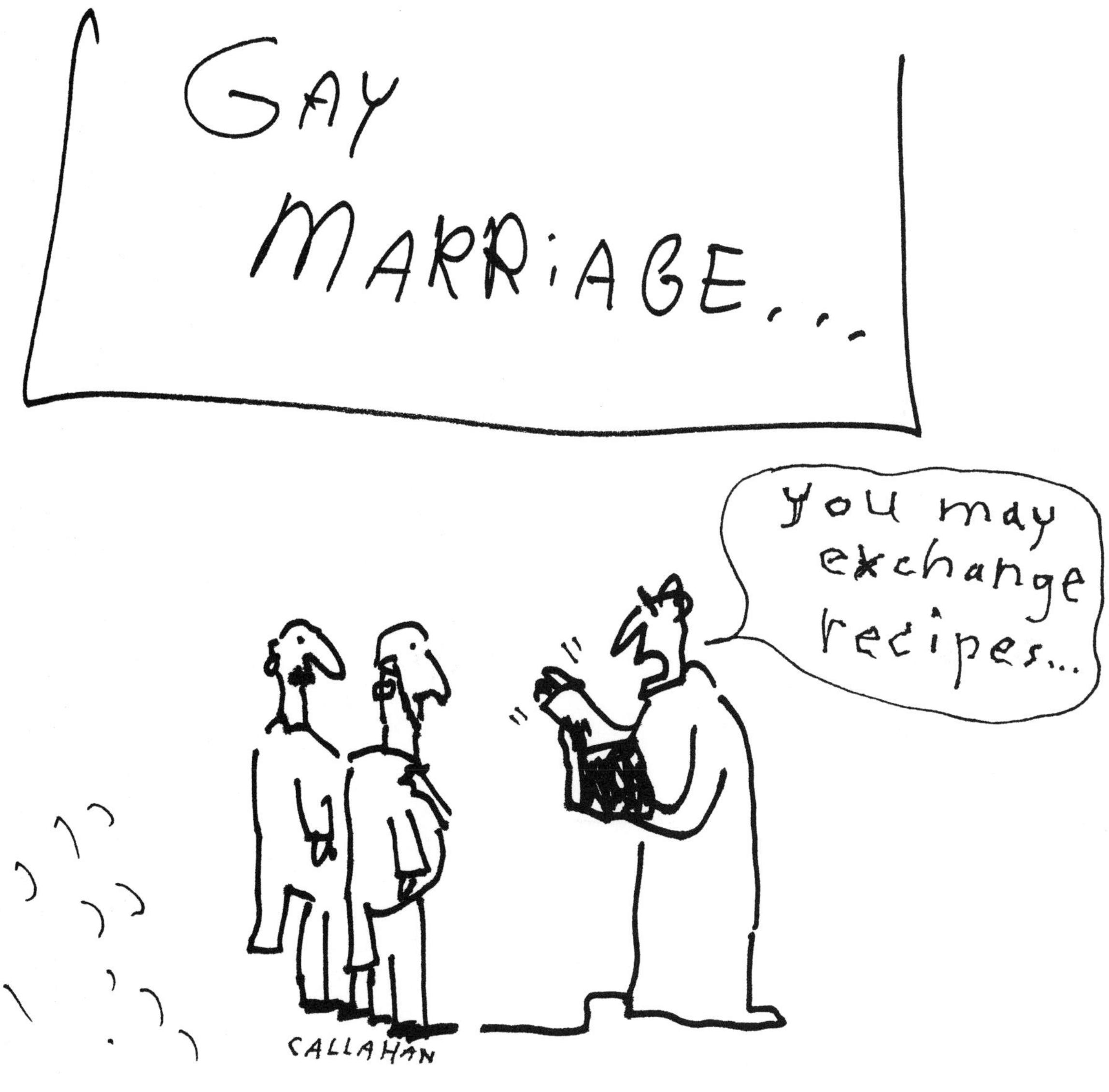
GAY MARRIAGE...
You may exchange recipes...
CALLAHAN

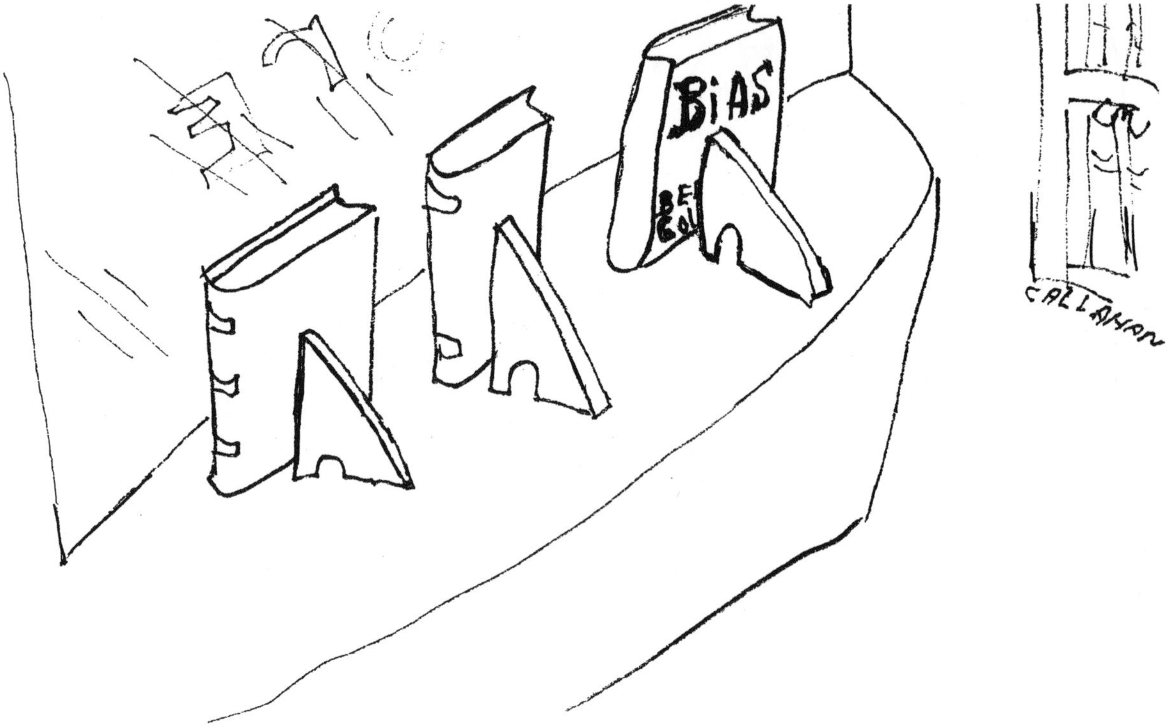
BiAS
CALLAHAN

Bernard Goldberg's contraversial book about media spin hits the stores...

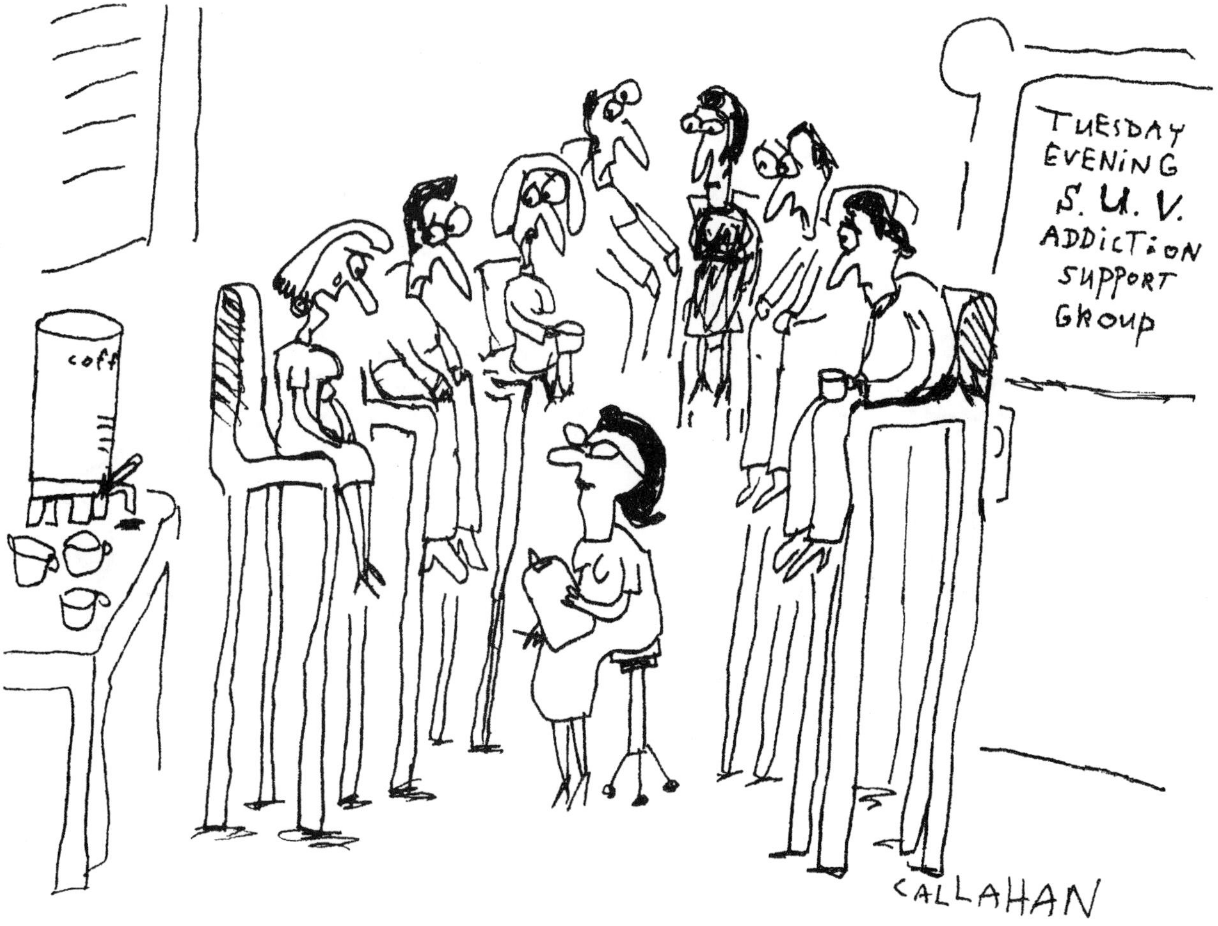
coff
TUESDAY EVENING S.U.V. ADDICTION SUPPORT GROUP
CALLAHAN

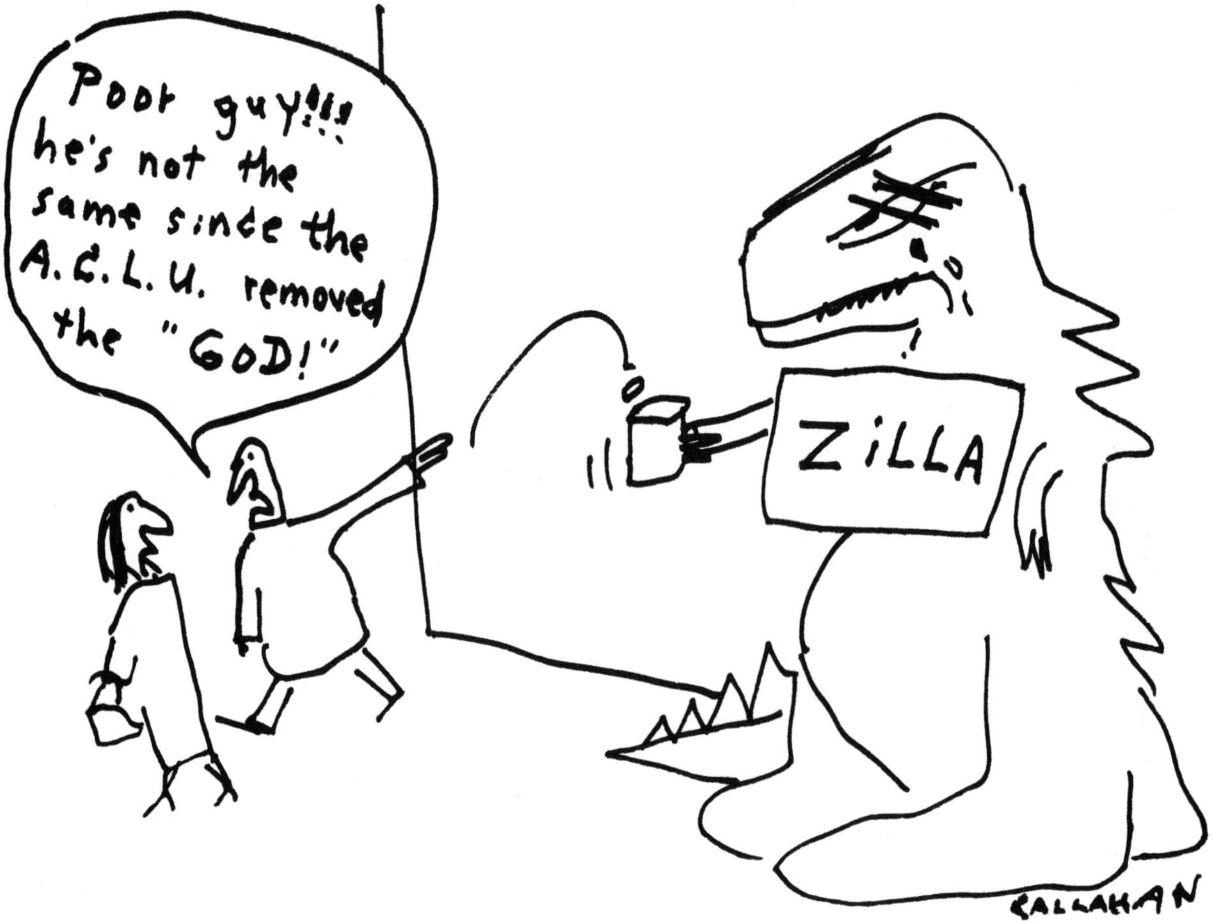
Poor guy!!! he's not the same since the A.C.L.U. removed the "GOD!"
ZiLLA
CALLAHAN

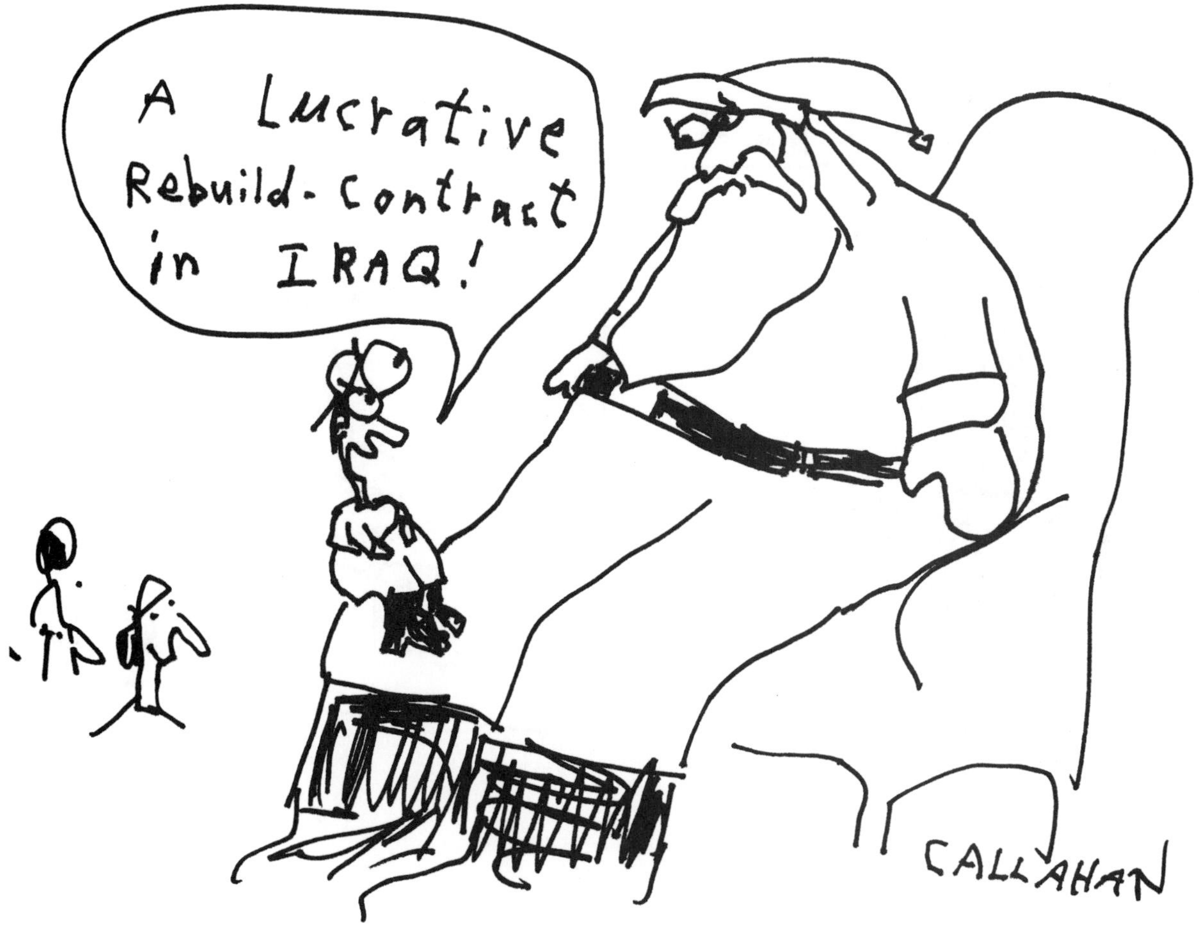
A Lucrative Rebuild-Contract in IRAQ!
CALLAHAN

Grandpa 1924
there I was... surrounded by Lions!!!
Grandpa 2004
there I was... surrounded by Pop-ups!
CALLAHAN

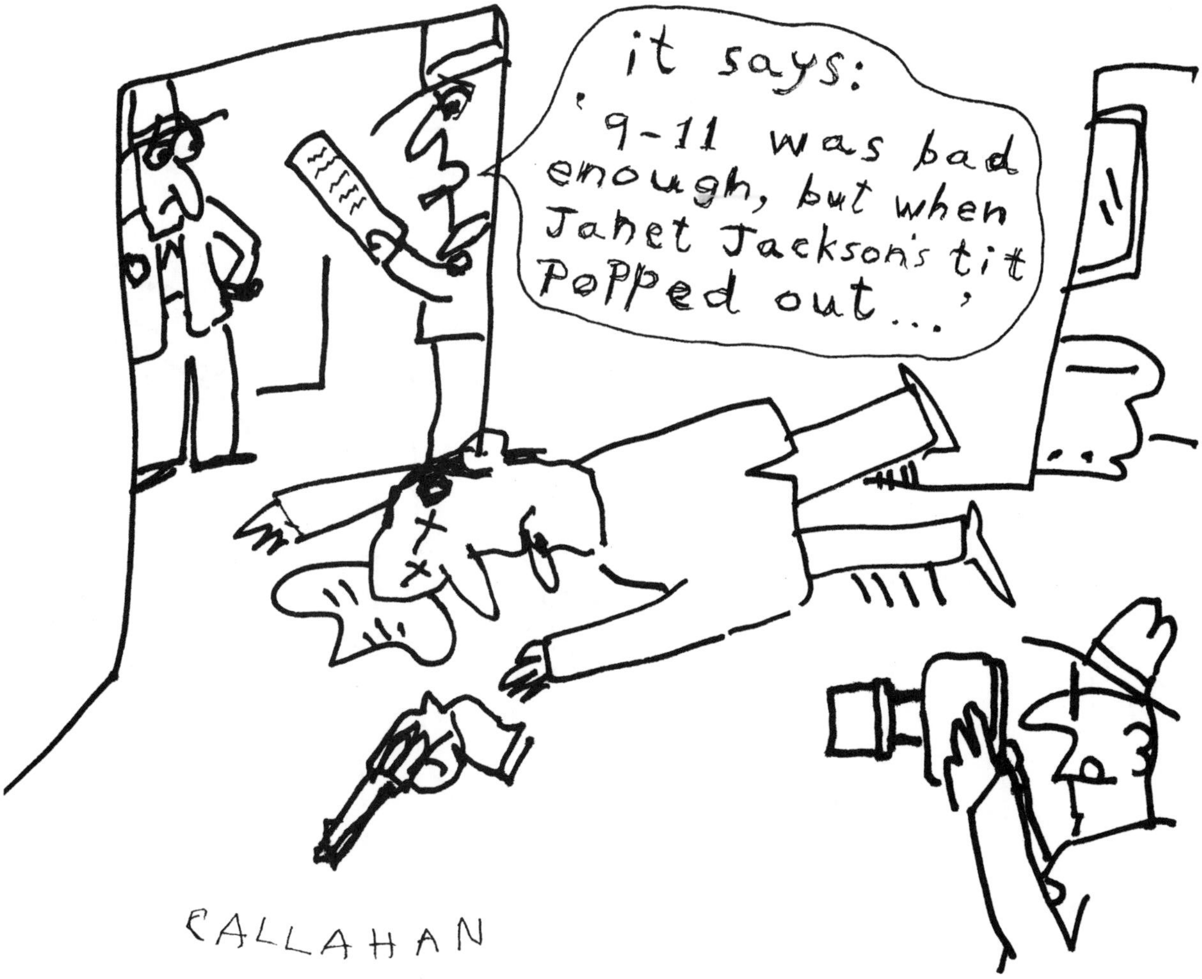
it says:
'9-11 was bad enough, but when Janet Jackson's tit popped out...'
CALLAHAN

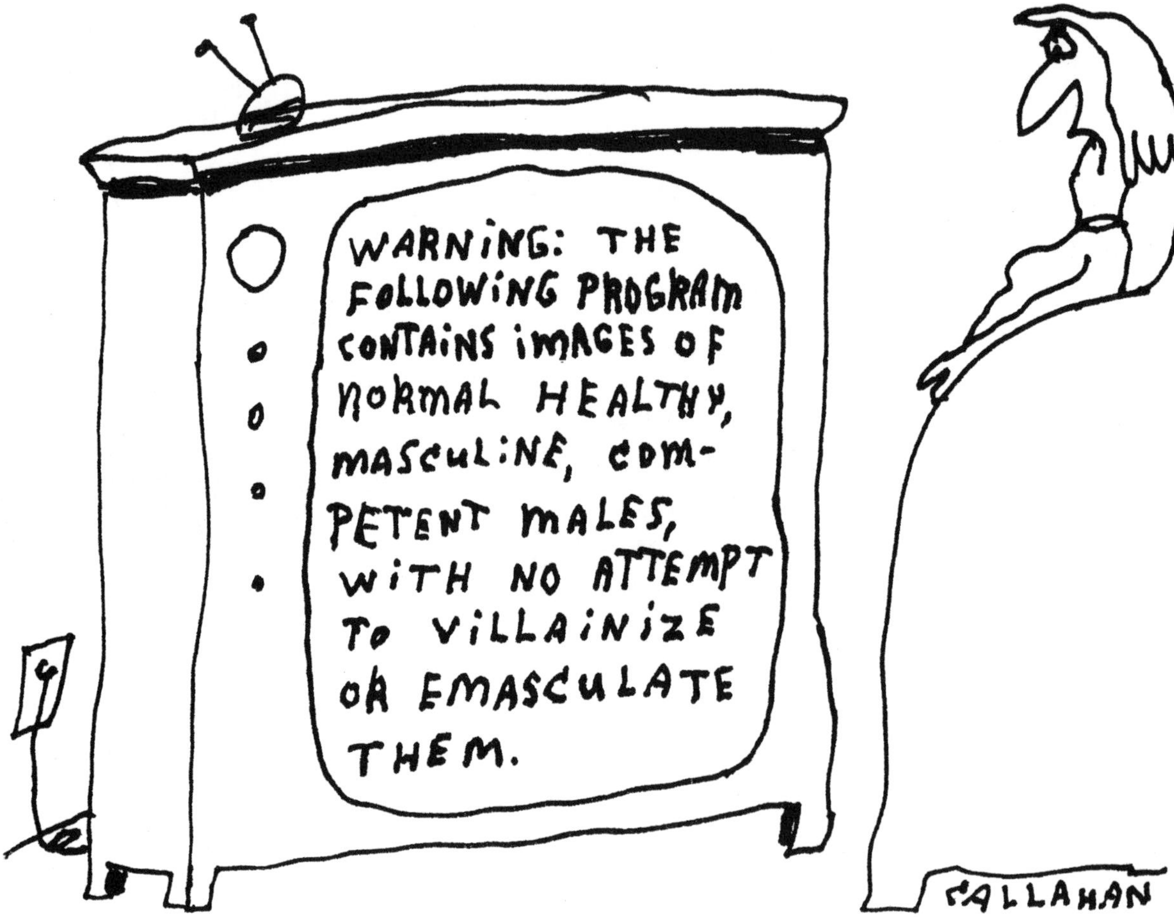
WARNING: THE FOLLOWING PROGRAM CONTAINS IMAGES OF NORMAL HEALTHY, MASCULINE, COM-PETENT MALES, WITH NO ATTEMPT TO VILLAINIZE OR EMASCULATE THEM.
CALLAHAN

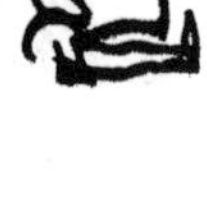

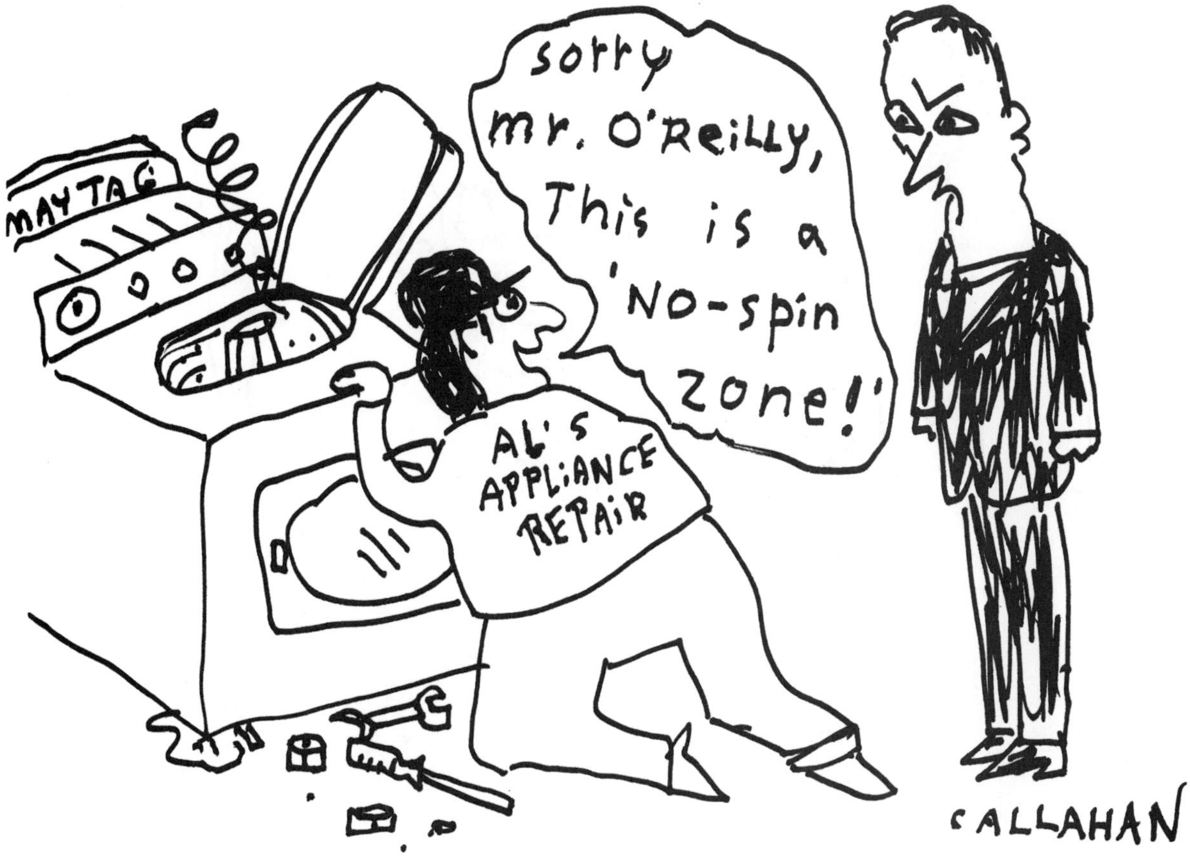
MAYTAG
sorry mr. O'Reilly, This is a 'No-spin zone!'
AL'S APPLIANCE REPAIR
CALLAHAN

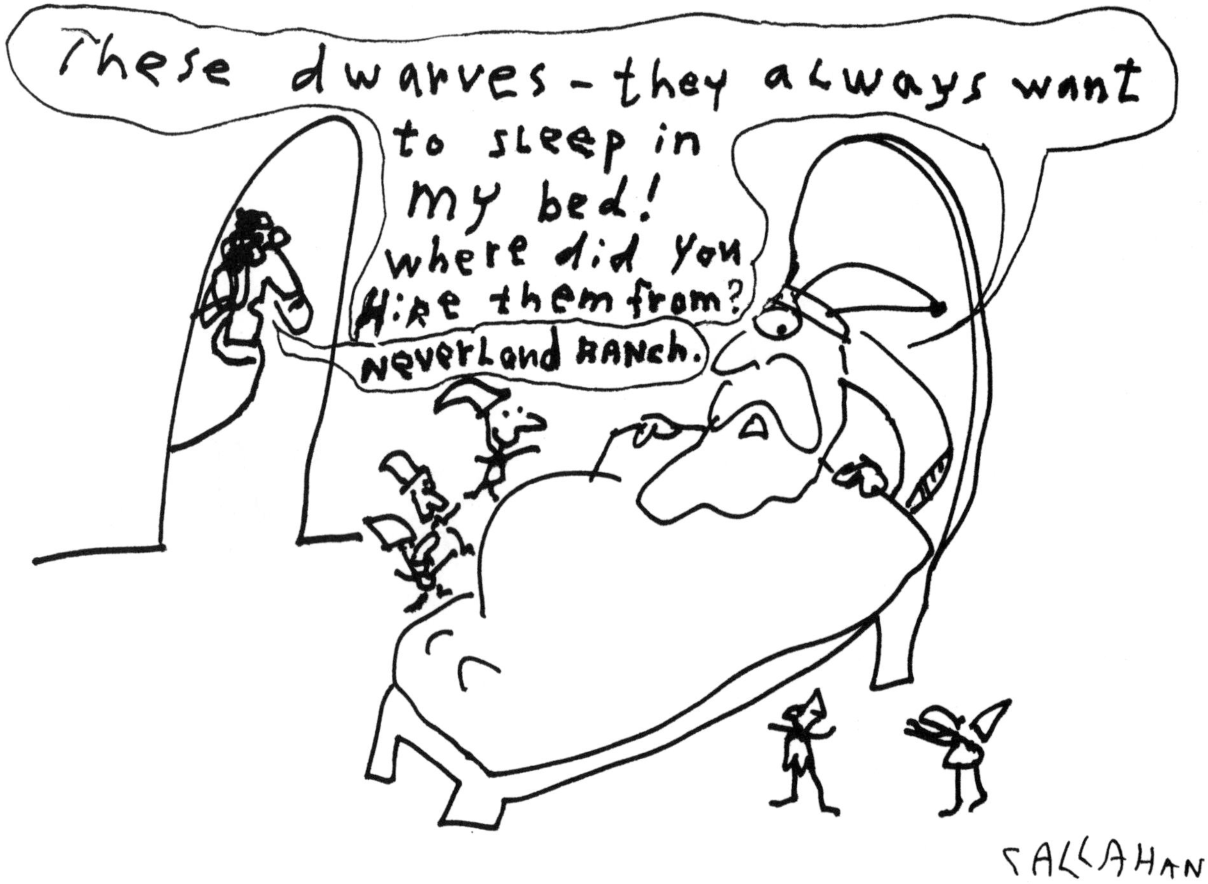
These dwarves - they always want to sleep in my bed! where did you Hire them from?
Neverland Ranch.
CALLAHAN

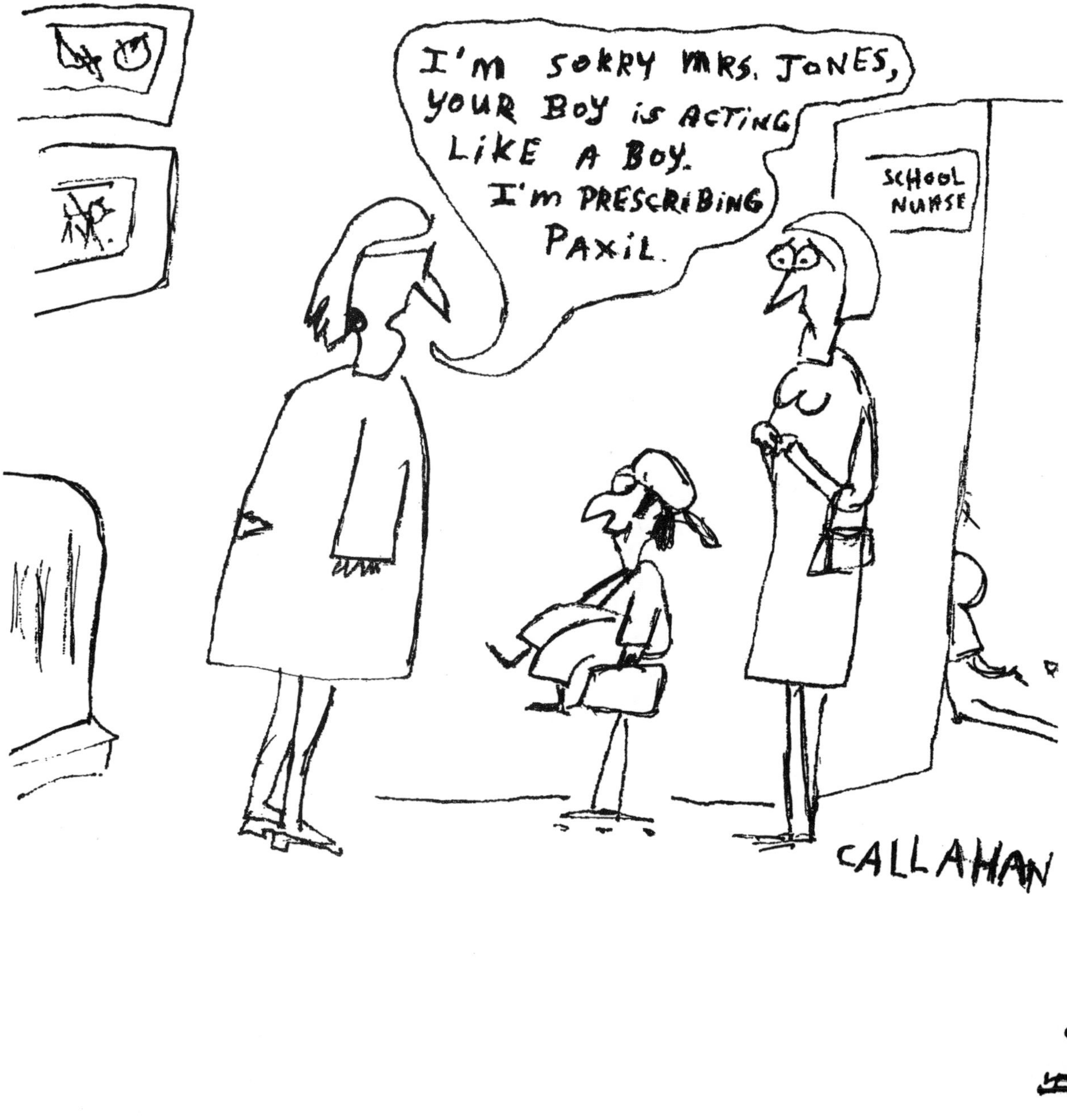
I'M SORRY MRS. JONES, YOUR BOY IS ACTING LIKE A BOY. I'M PRESCRIBING PAXIL.
SCHOOL NURSE
CALLAHAN

STOP STARING AT MY BREASTS
STOP STARING AT MY WALLET!
CALLAHAN

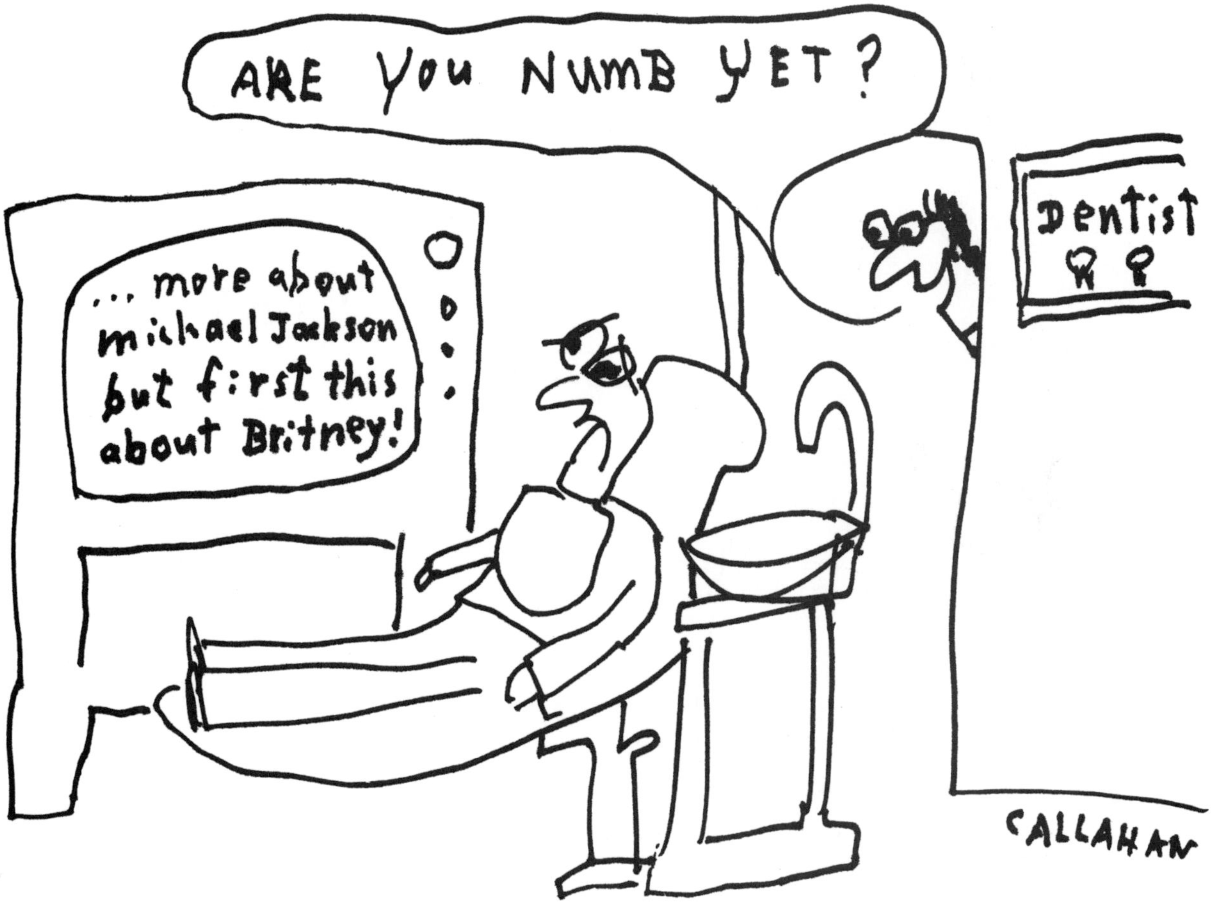
ARE YOU NUMB YET?
... more about michael Jackson but first this about Britney!
Dentist
CALLAHAN

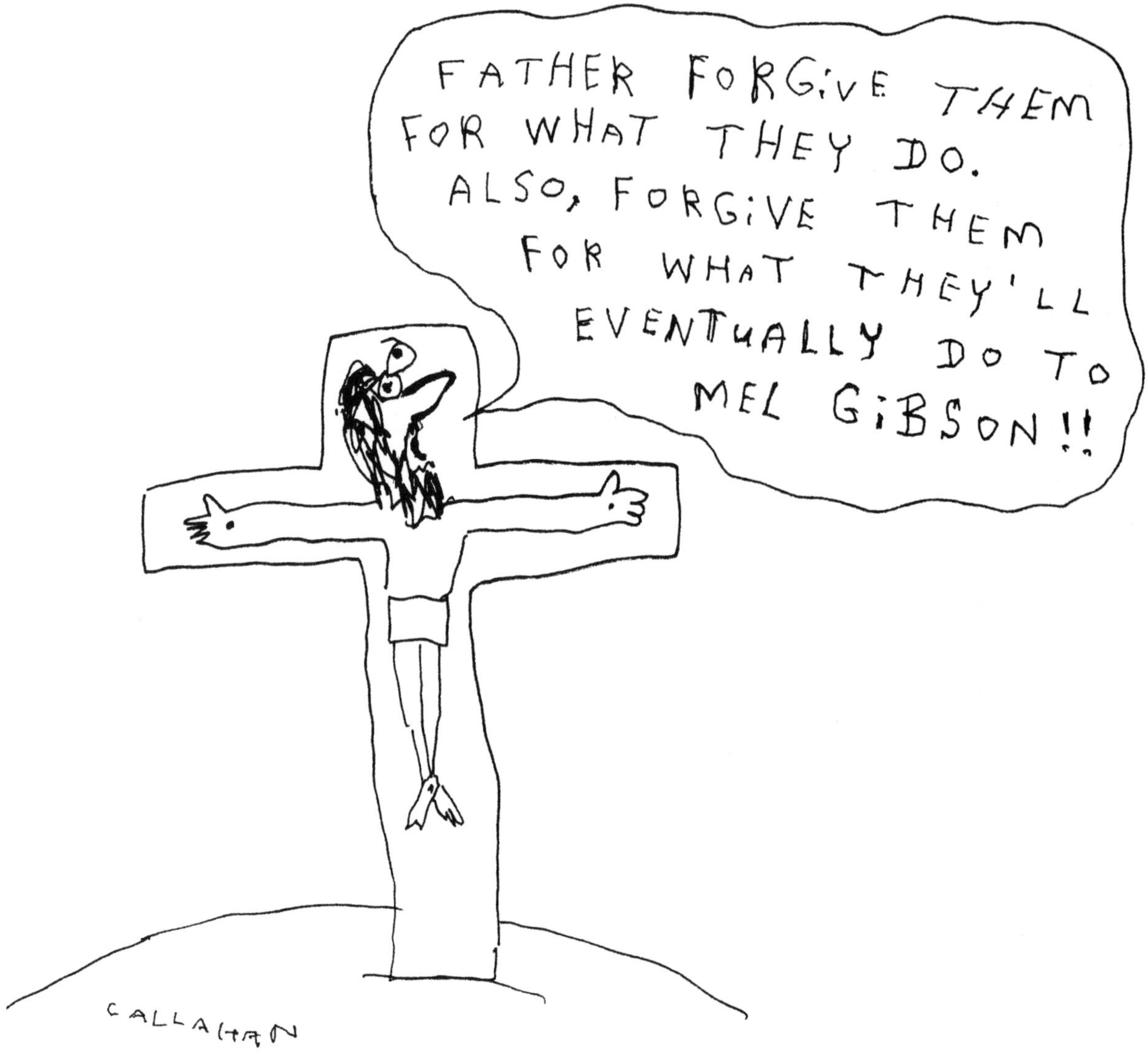
FATHER FORGIVE THEM FOR WHAT THEY DO. ALSO, FORGIVE THEM FOR WHAT THEY'LL EVENTUALLY DO TO MEL GIBSON!!
CALLAHAN

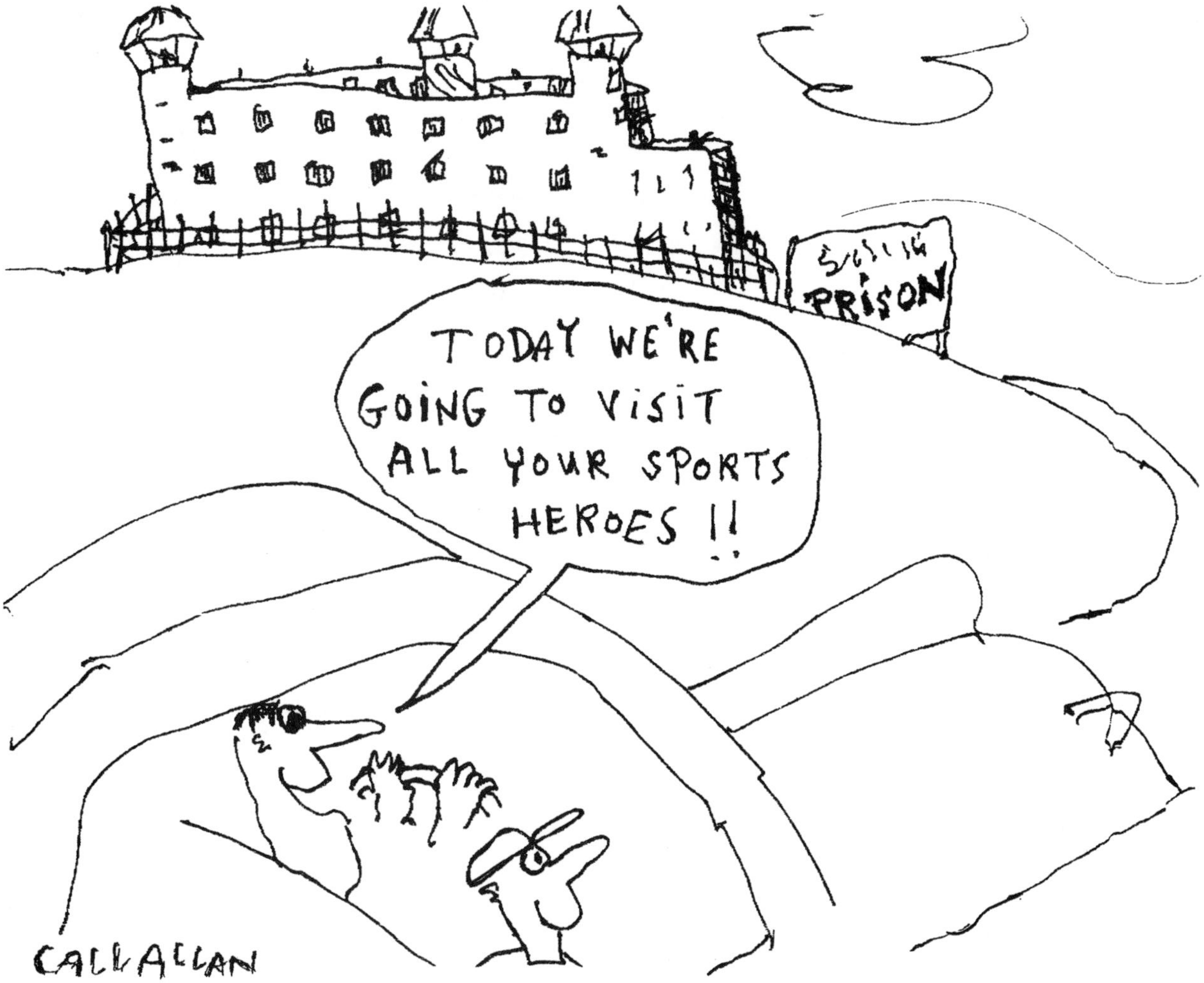
PRISON
TODAY WE'RE GOING TO VISIT ALL YOUR SPORTS HEROES !!
CALLAHAN

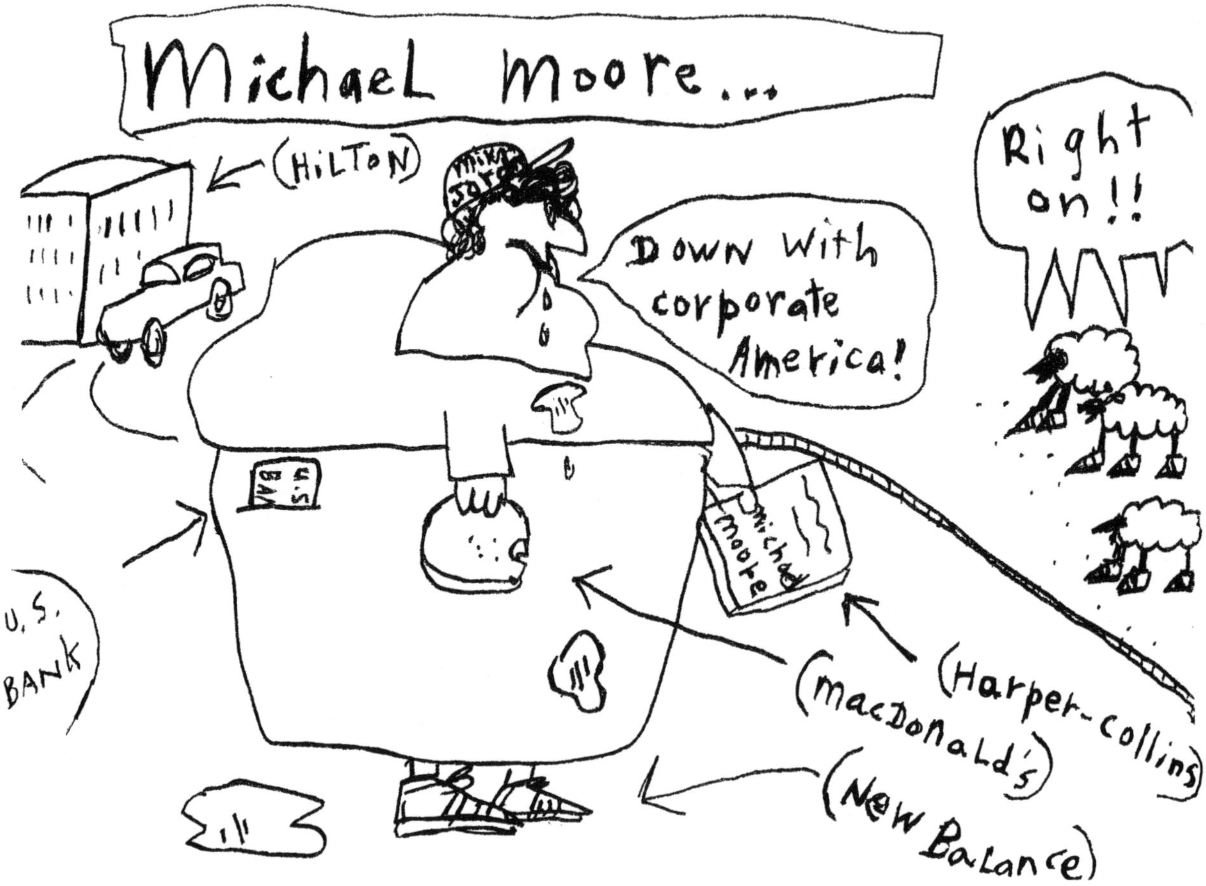

Michael moore...
(HILTON)
Down with corporate America!
Right on!!
Michael Moore
U.S. BANK
(Harper-collins)
(macDonald's)
(New Balance)

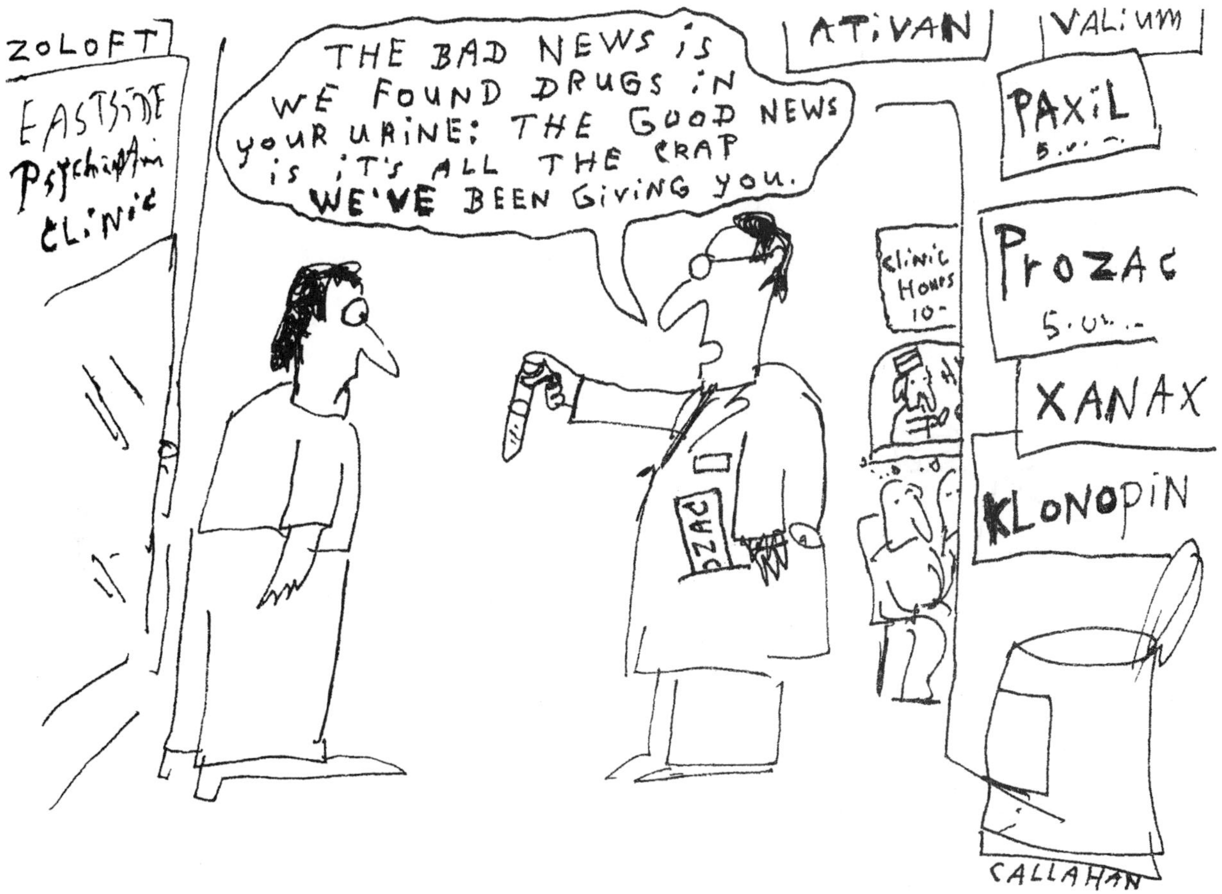
THE BAD NEWS IS WE FOUND DRUGS IN YOUR URINE; THE GOOD NEWS IS IT'S ALL THE CRAP WE'VE BEEN GIVING YOU.
ZOLOFT
EASTSIDE
CLINIC
ATIVAN
VALIUM
PAXIL
PROZAC
XANAX
KLONOPIN
CALLAHAN

A brain for the straw man, courage for the lion, a heart for the tin man, and a sense of humor for the feminists.
CALLAHAN

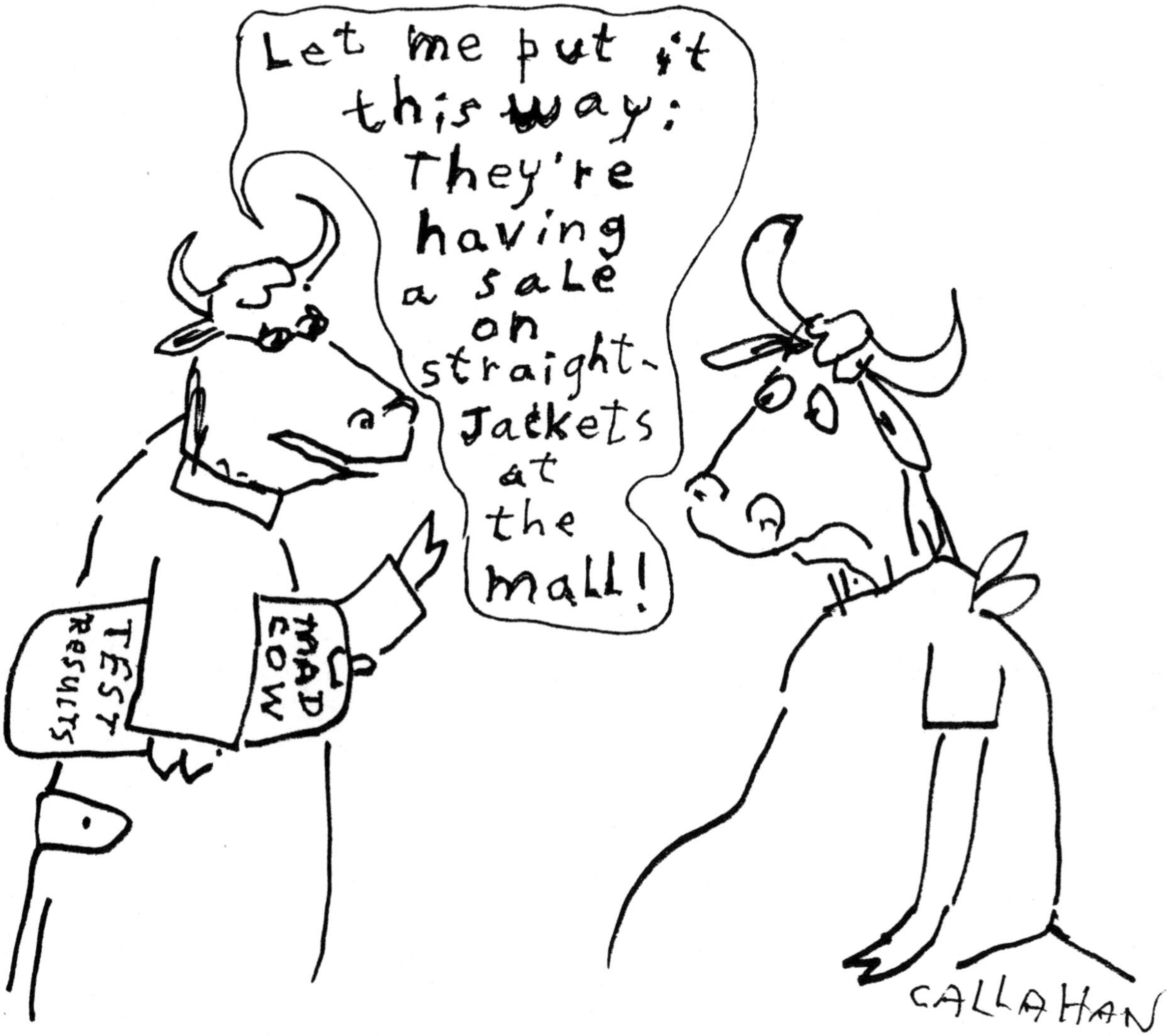
Let me put it this way: They're having a sale on straight-Jackets at the mall!
TEST RESULTS
MAD COW
CALLAHAN

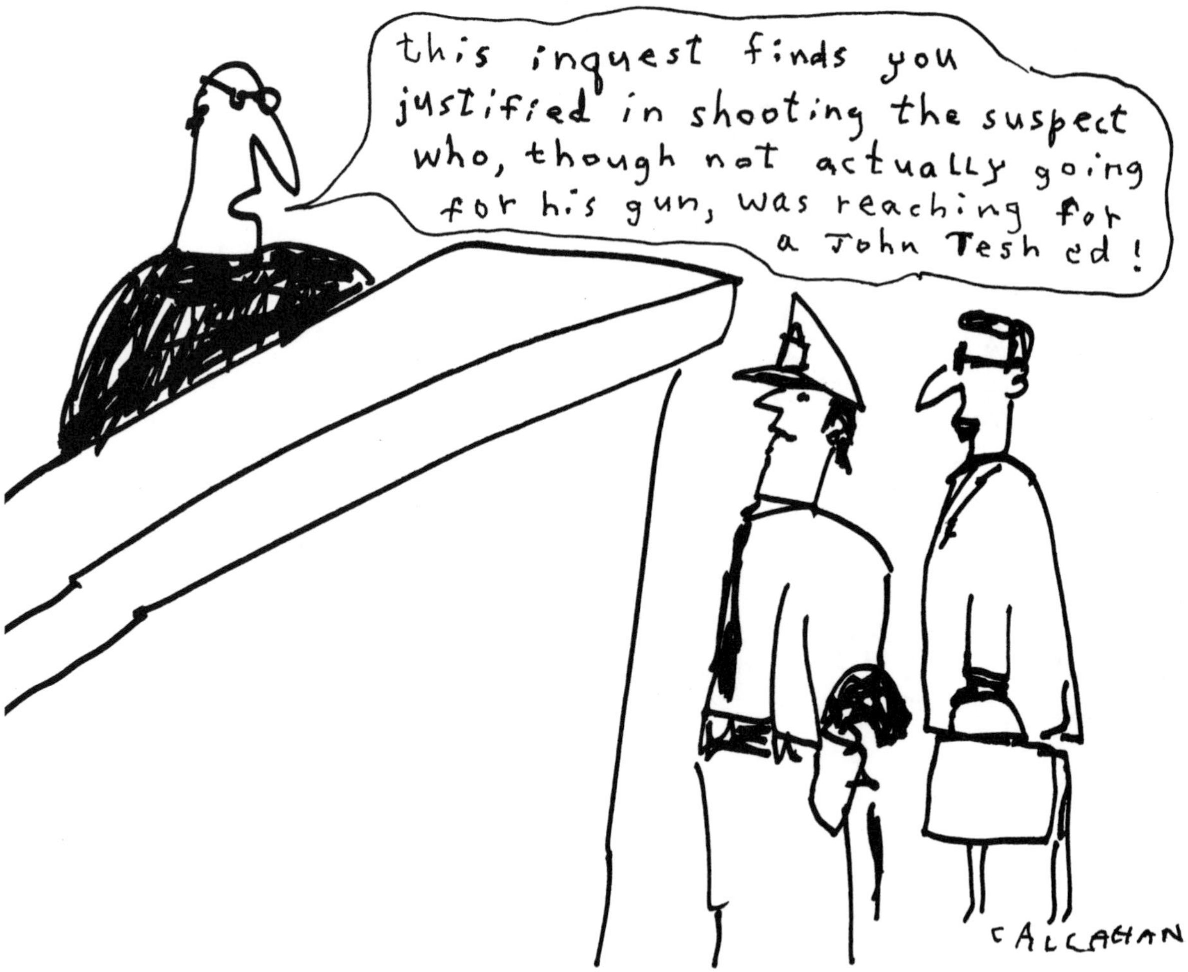
this inquest finds you justified in shooting the suspect who, though not actually going for his gun, was reaching for a John Tesh cd!
CALLAHAN

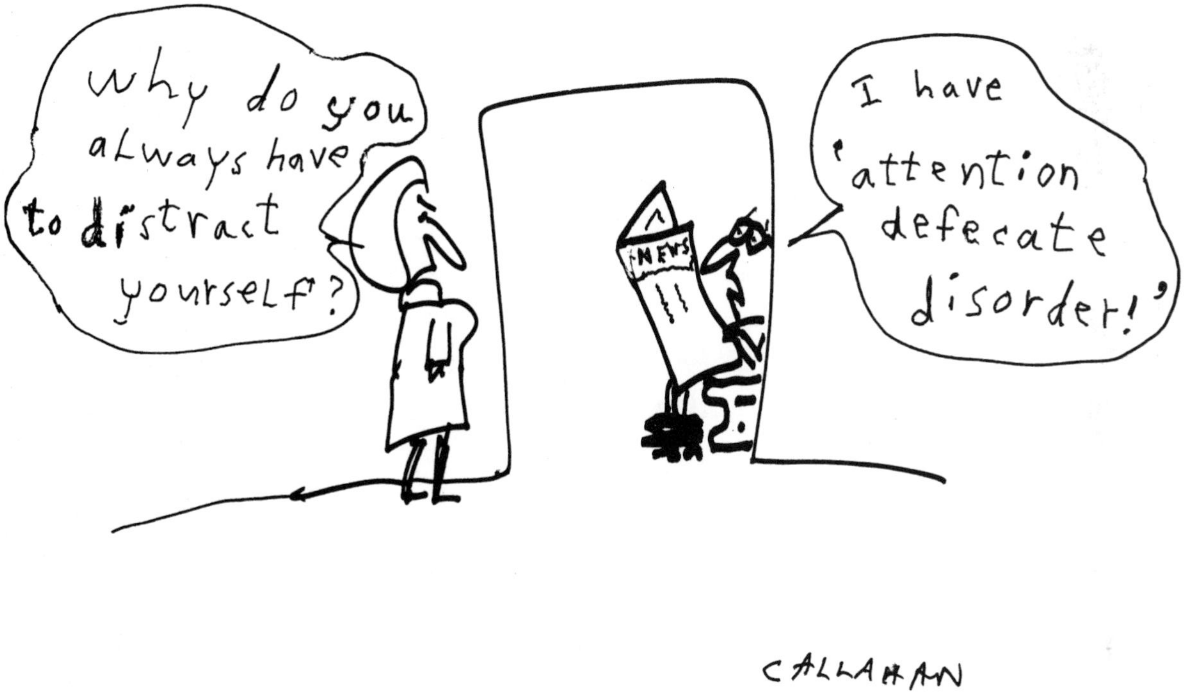
why do you always have to distract yourself?
I have 'attention defecate disorder!'
NEWS
CALLAHAN

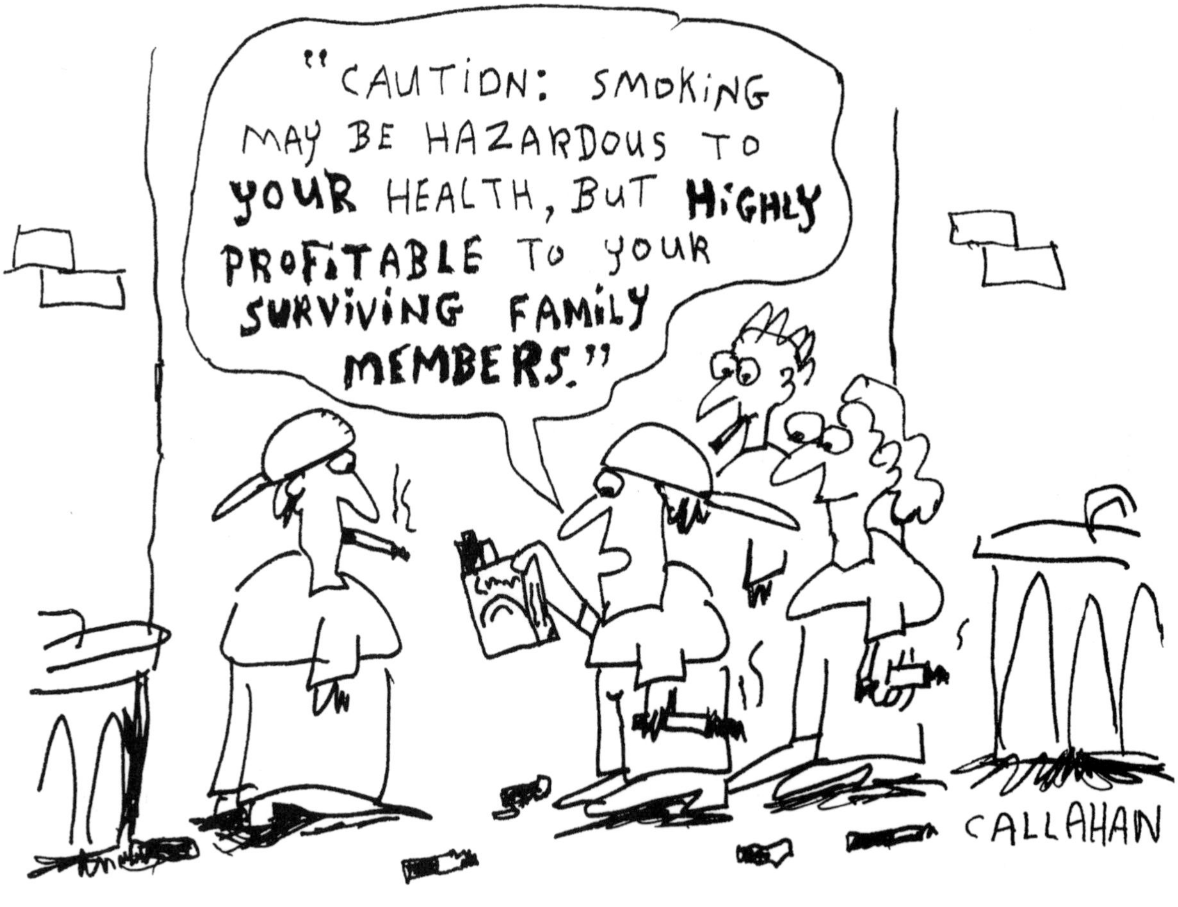
"CAUTION: SMOKING MAY BE HAZARDOUS TO YOUR HEALTH, BUT HIGHLY PROFITABLE TO YOUR SURVIVING FAMILY MEMBERS."
CALLAHAN

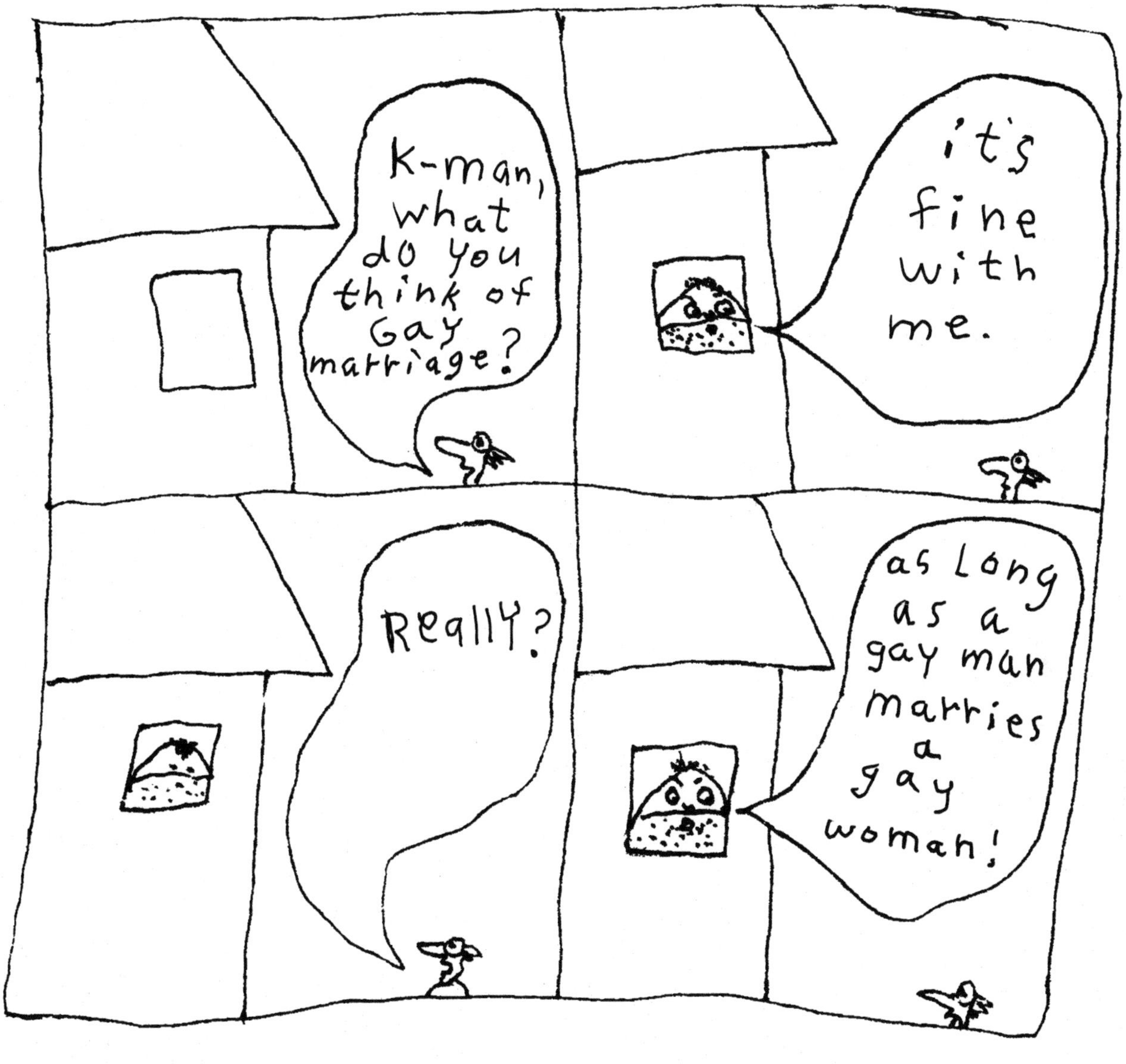
K-man, what do you think of gay marriage?
it's fine with me.
Really?
as long as a gay man marries a gay woman!

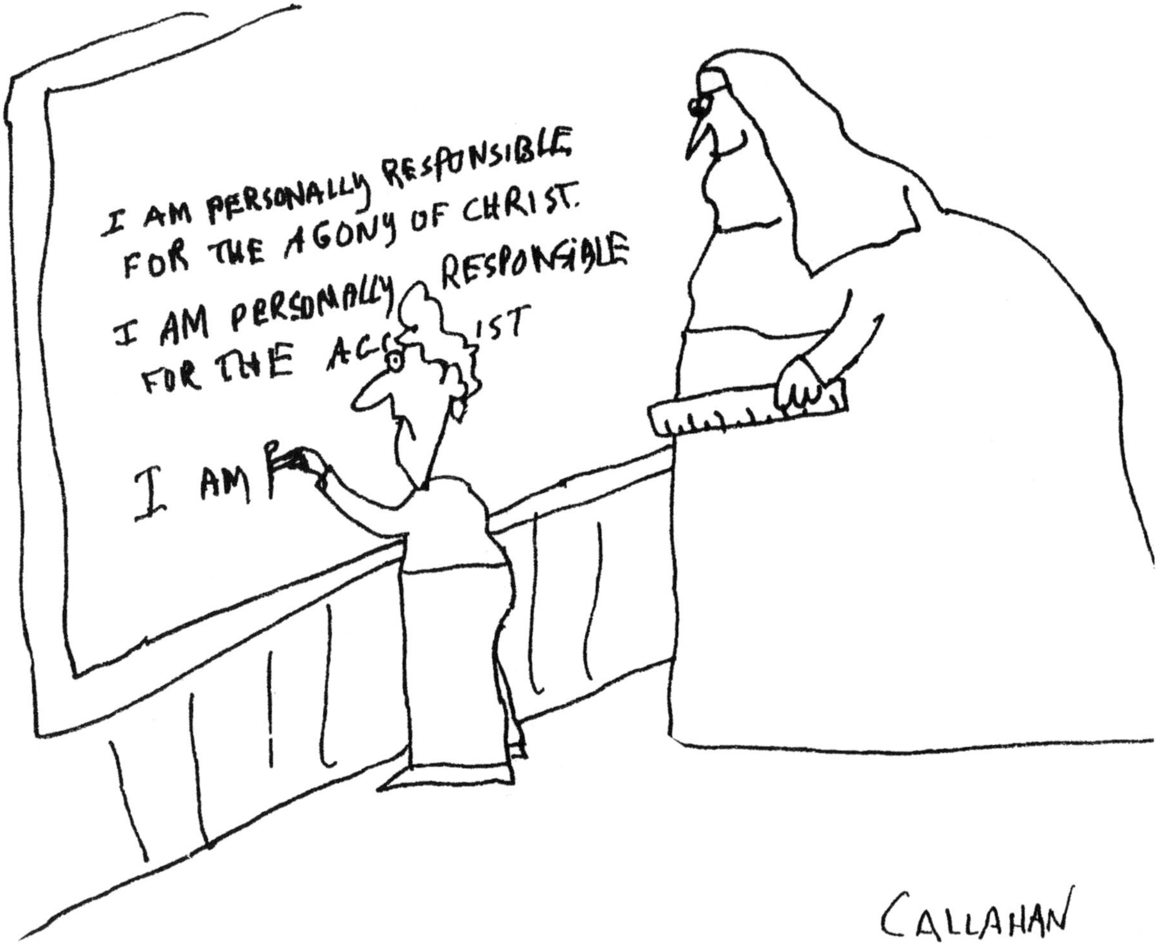
I AM PERSONALLY RESPONSIBLE FOR THE AGONY OF CHRIST.
I AM PERSONALLY RESPONSIBLE FOR THE AC IST
I AM
CALLAHAN

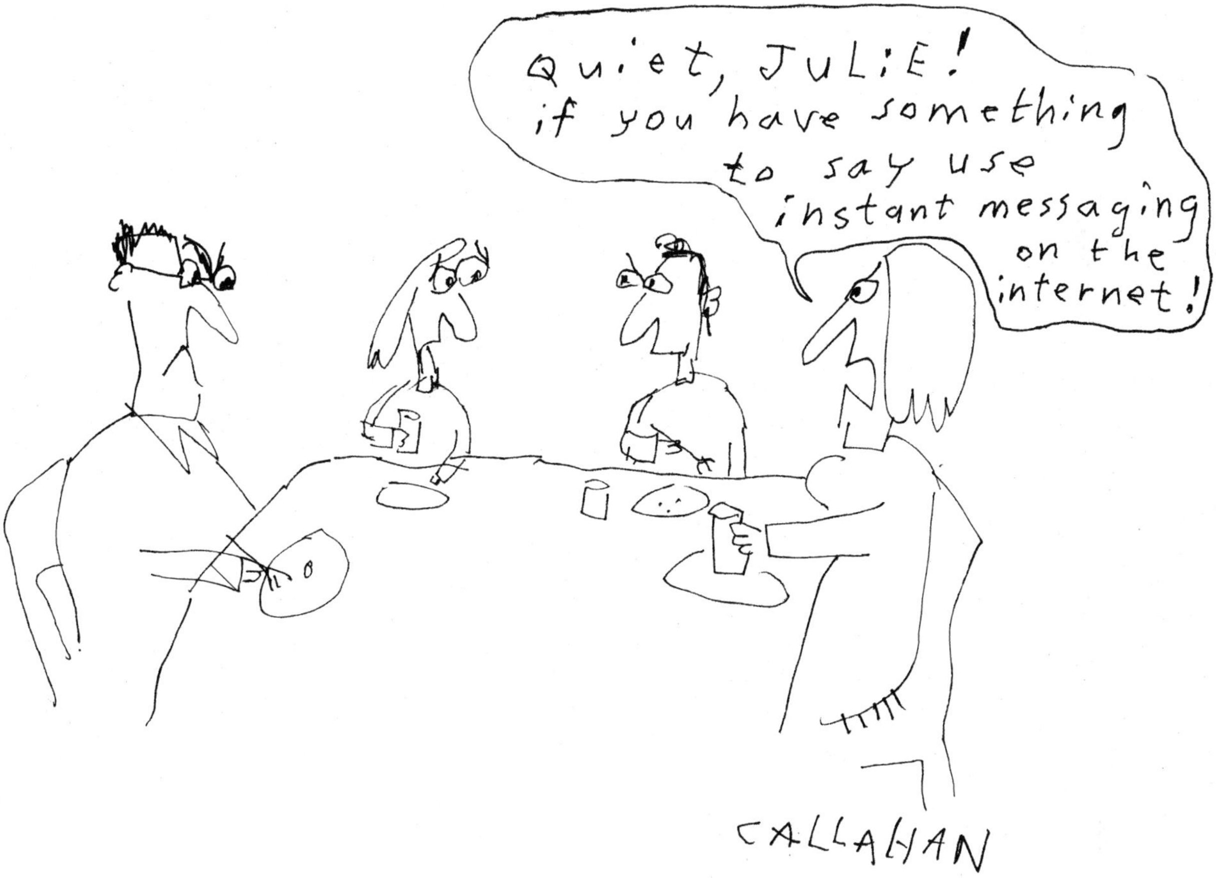
Quiet, JULiE! if you have something to say use instant messaging on the internet!
CALLAHAN

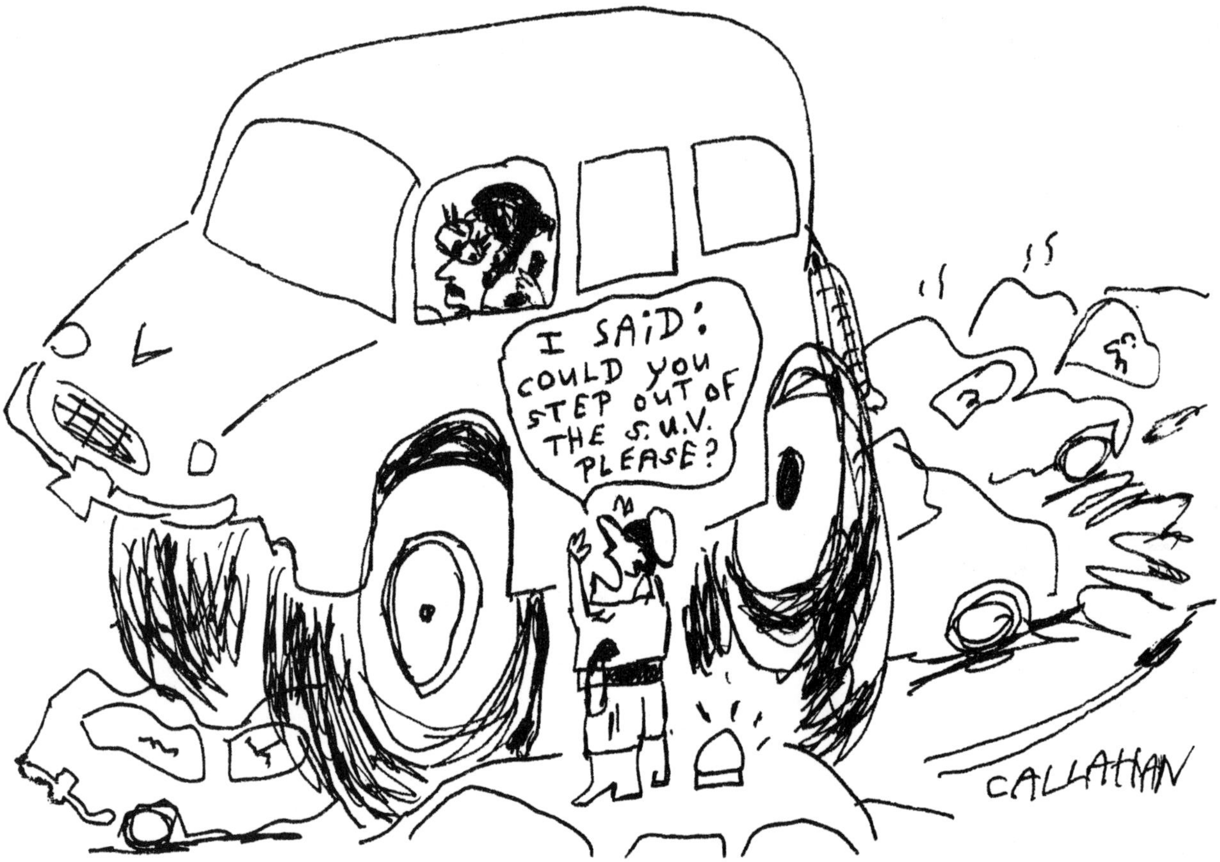
I SAID: COULD YOU STEP OUT OF THE S.U.V. PLEASE?
CALLAHAN

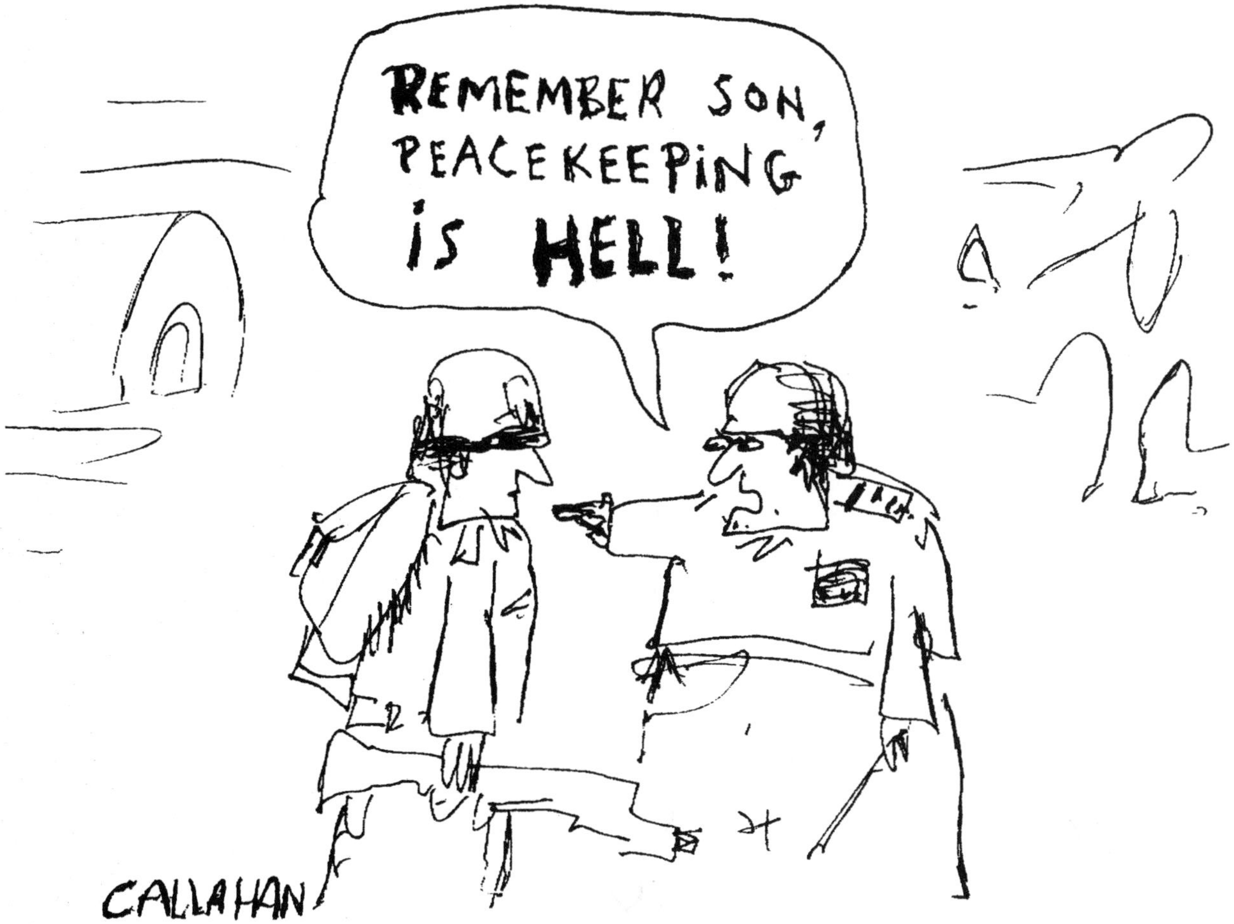
REMEMBER SON,
PEACEKEEPING
IS HELL!
CALLAHAN

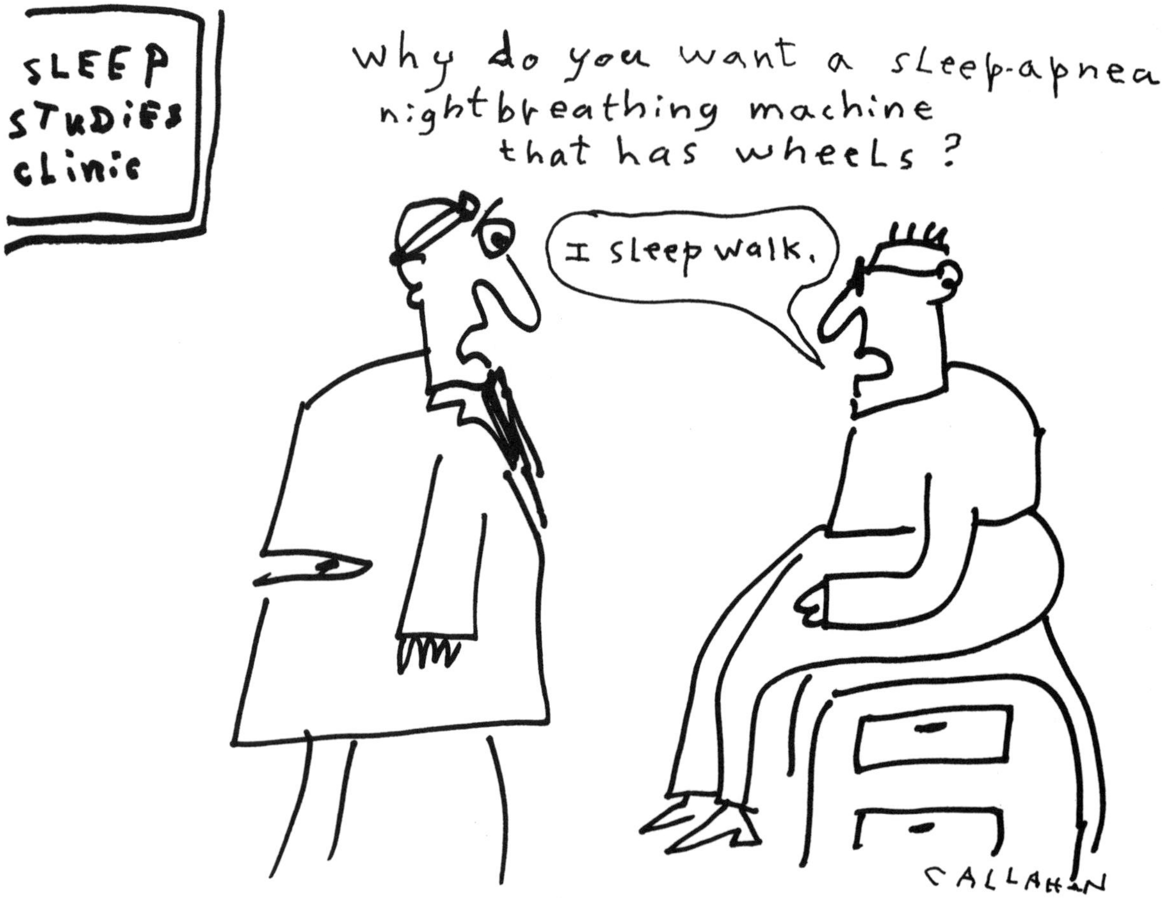
SLEEP STUDIES CLINIC
I sleep walk.
CALLAHAN

Why do you want a sleep-apnea nightbreathing machine that has wheels?

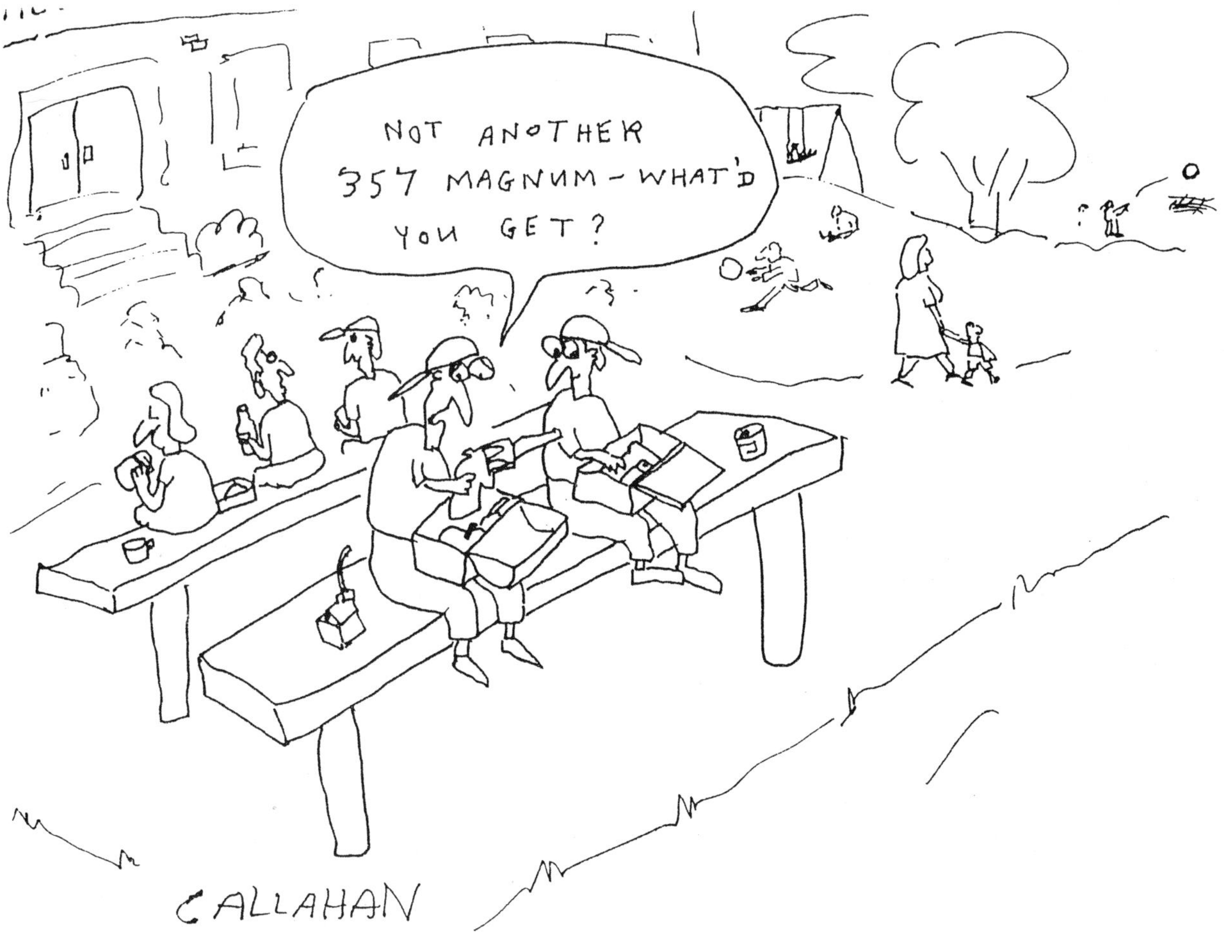
NOT ANOTHER 357 MAGNUM - WHAT'D YOU GET?
CALLAHAN

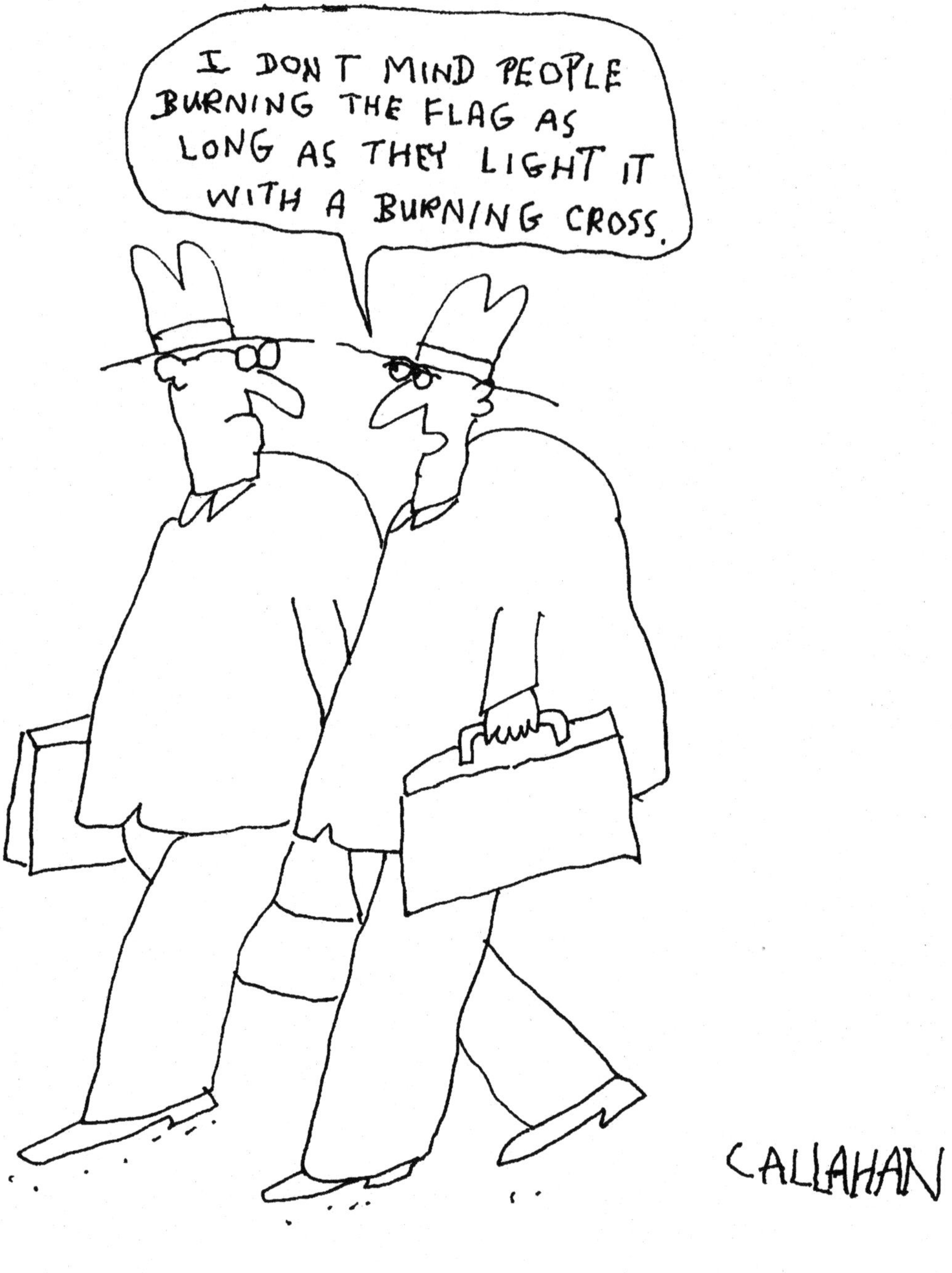
I DONT MIND PEOPLE BURNING THE FLAG AS LONG AS THEY LIGHT IT WITH A BURNING CROSS.
CALLAHAN

THE PASSION OF MEL GIBSON...

BANK

CALLAHAN

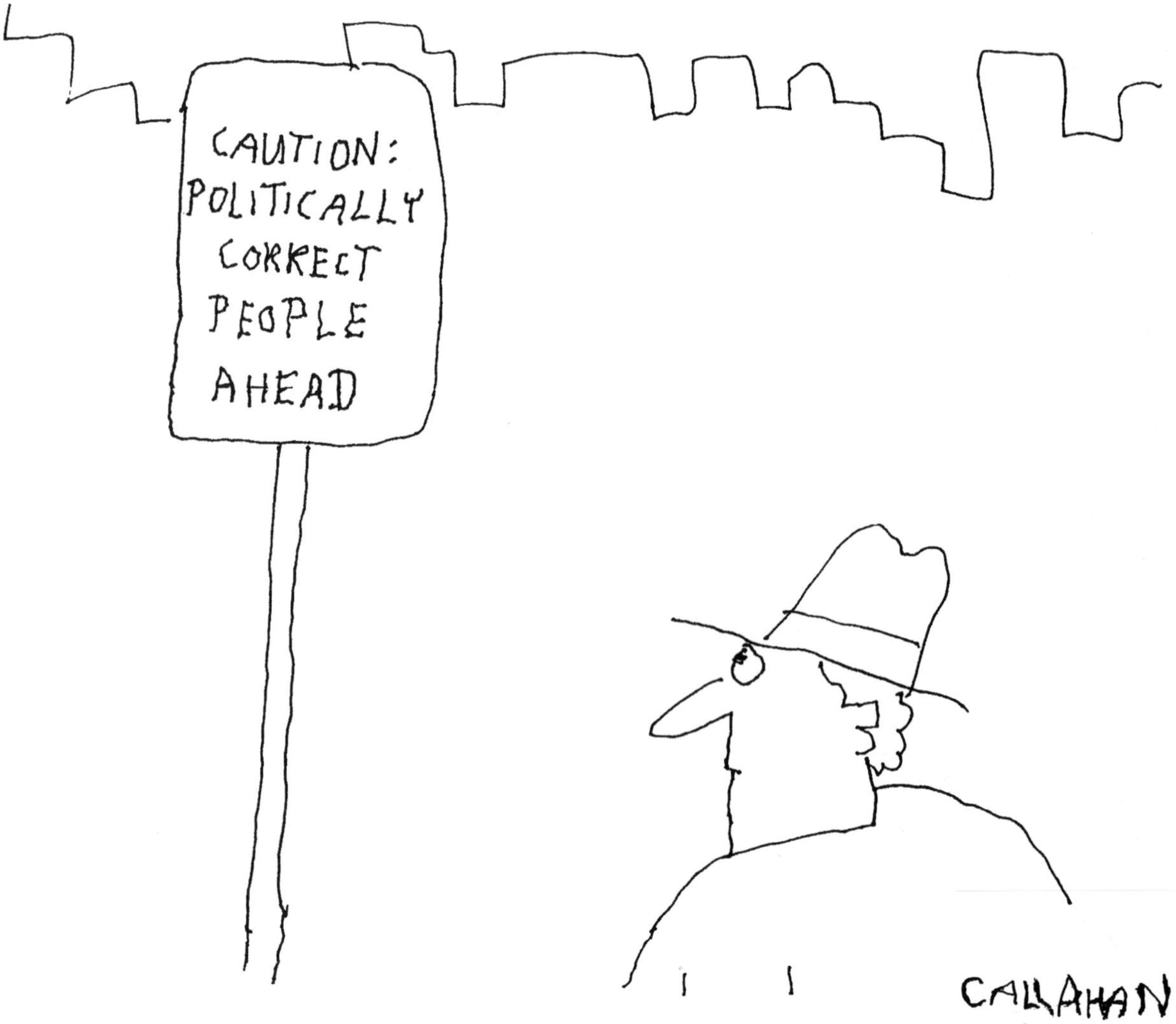
CAUTION: POLITICALLY CORRECT PEOPLE AHEAD
CALLAHAN

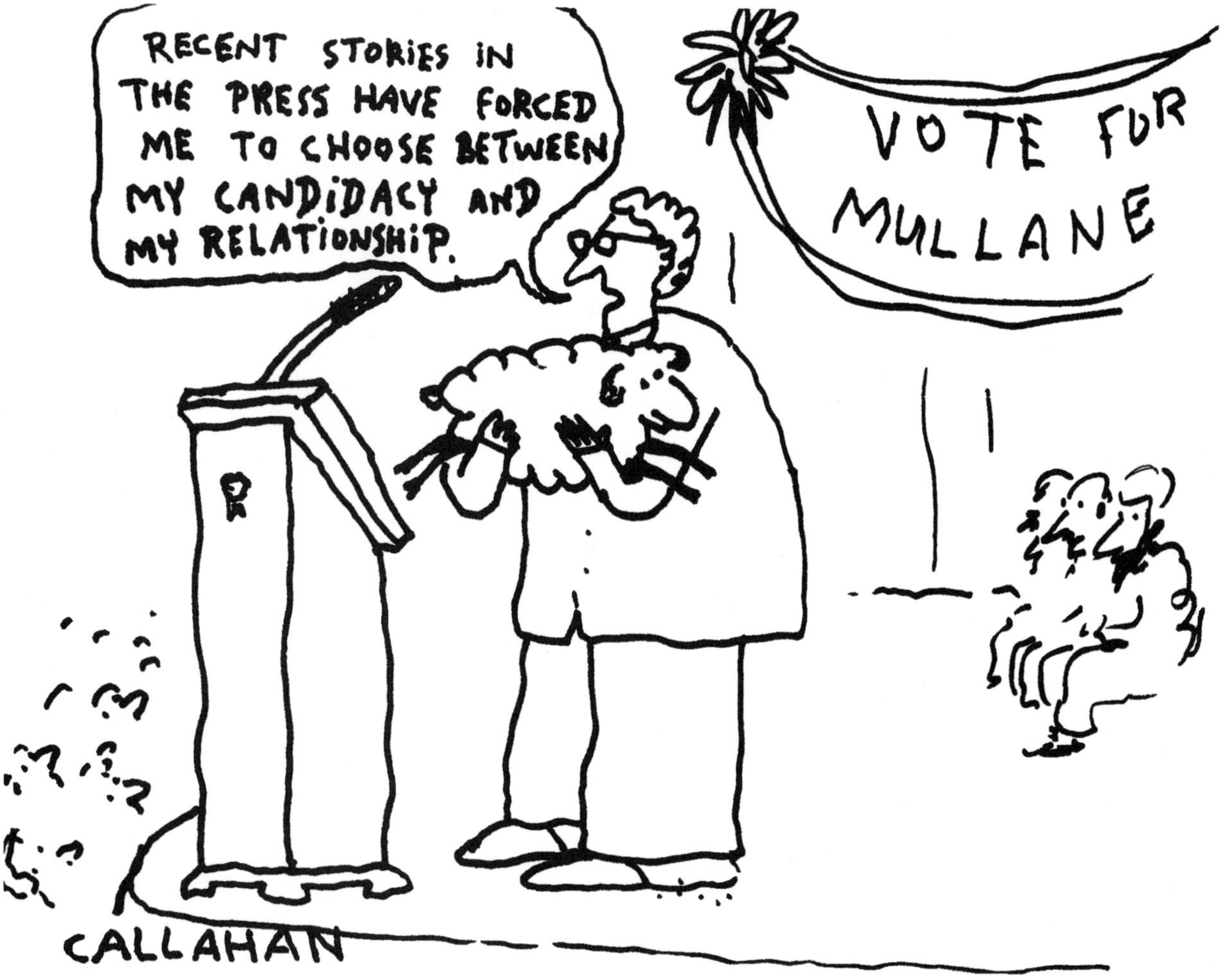
RECENT STORIES IN THE PRESS HAVE FORCED ME TO CHOOSE BETWEEN MY CANDIDACY AND MY RELATIONSHIP.
VOTE FOR MULLANE
CALLAHAN

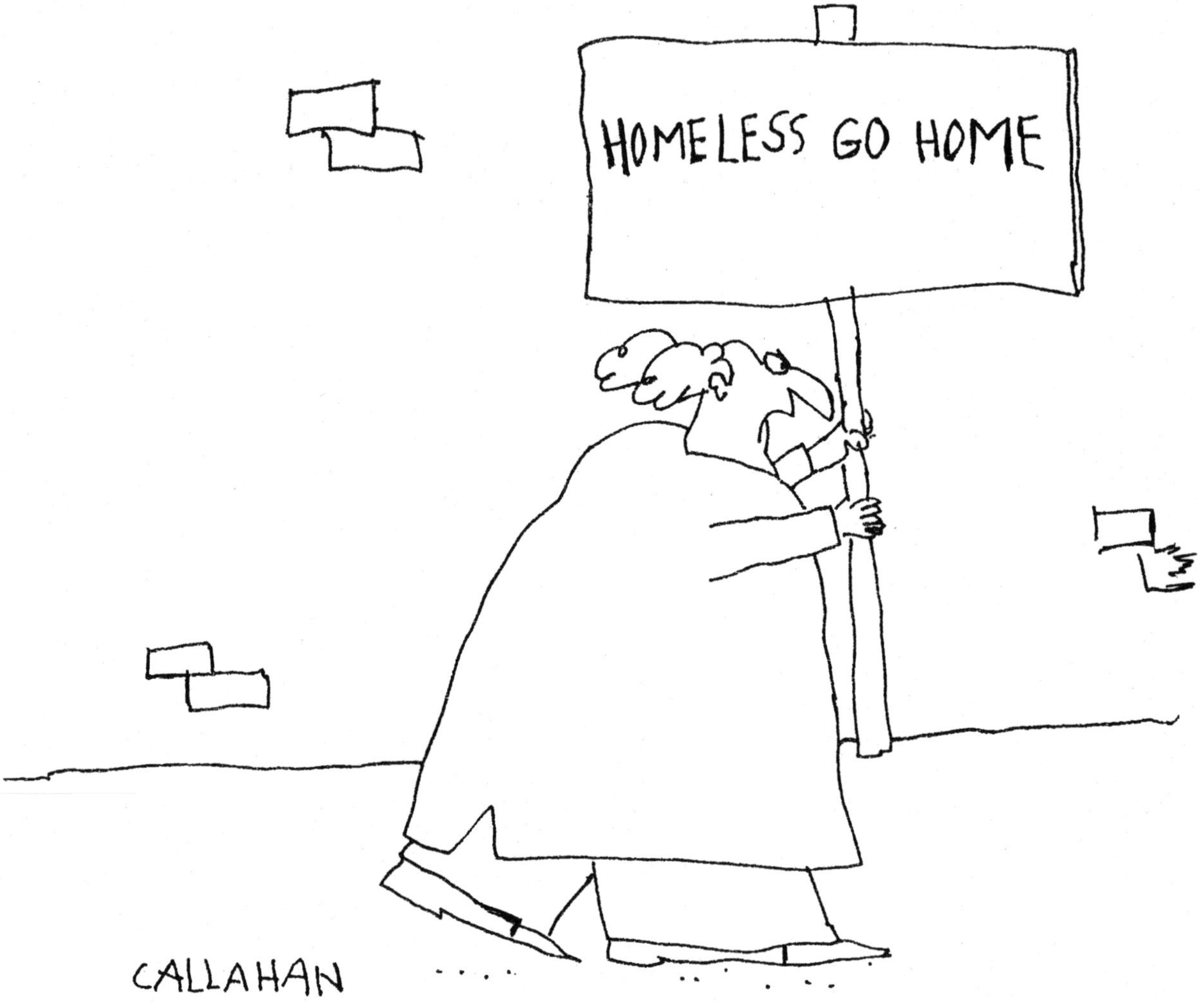
HOMELESS GO HOME
CALLAHAN

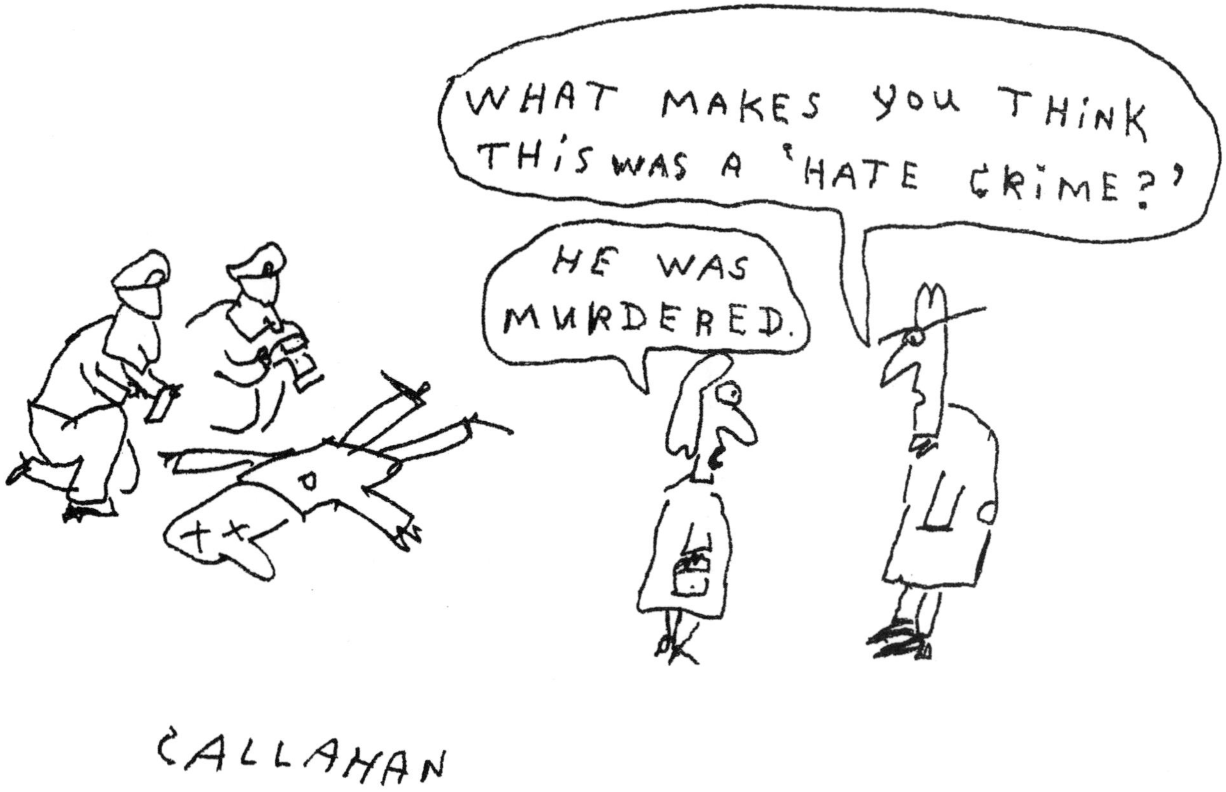
WHAT MAKES YOU THINK THIS WAS A 'HATE CRIME?'
HE WAS MURDERED.
CALLAHAN

WANTED
FOR
DEPRESSION
WANTED
FOR
MURDER

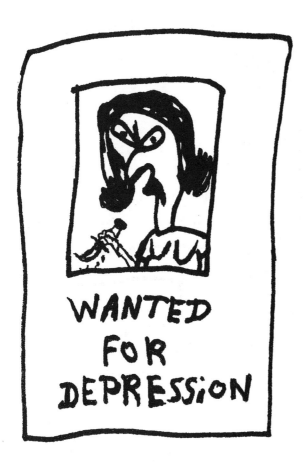

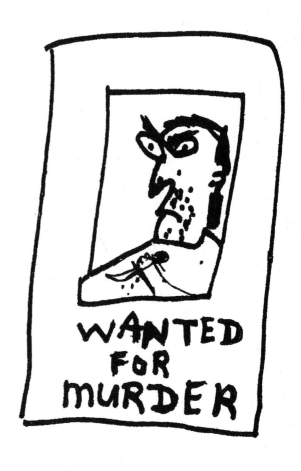

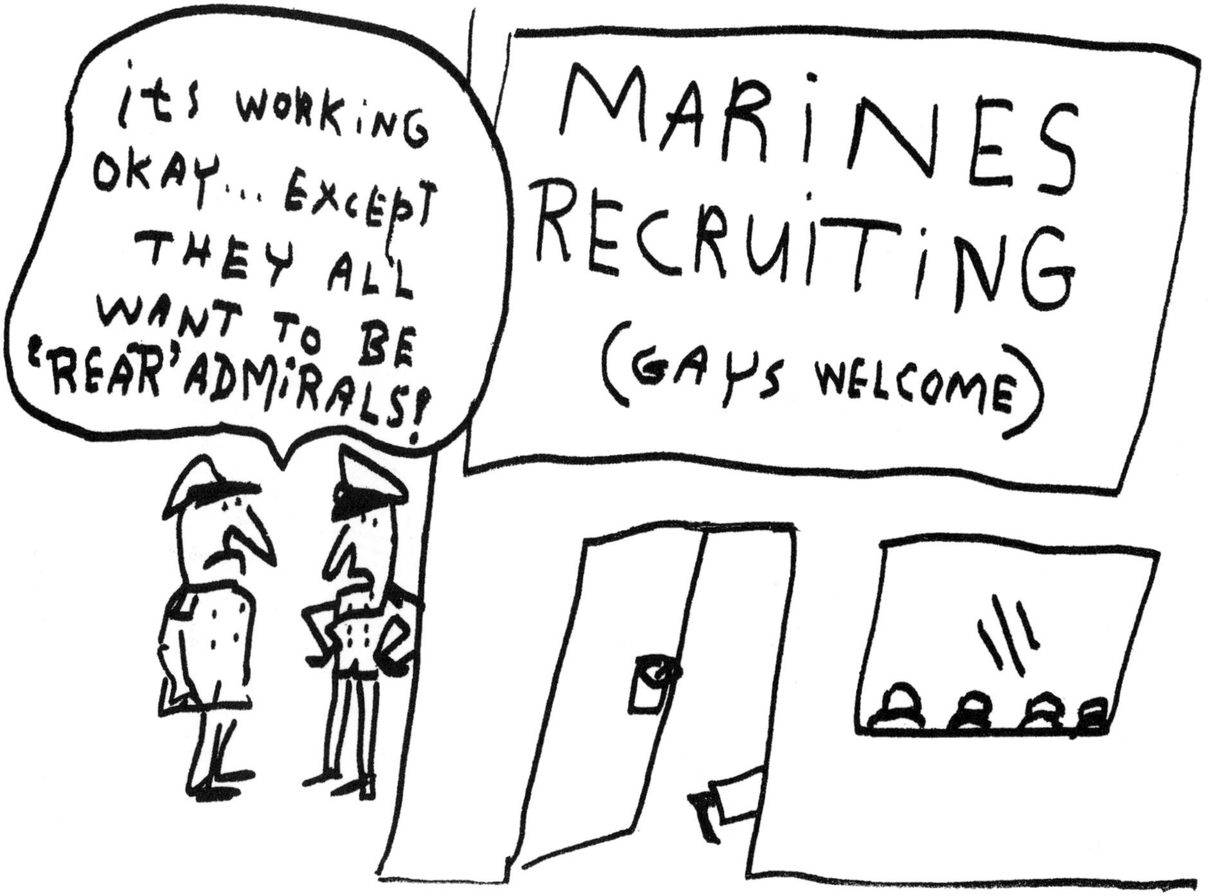
ITS WORKING OKAY... EXCEPT THEY ALL WANT TO BE 'REAR' ADMIRALS!
MARINES RECRUITING
(GAYS WELCOME)
SIM

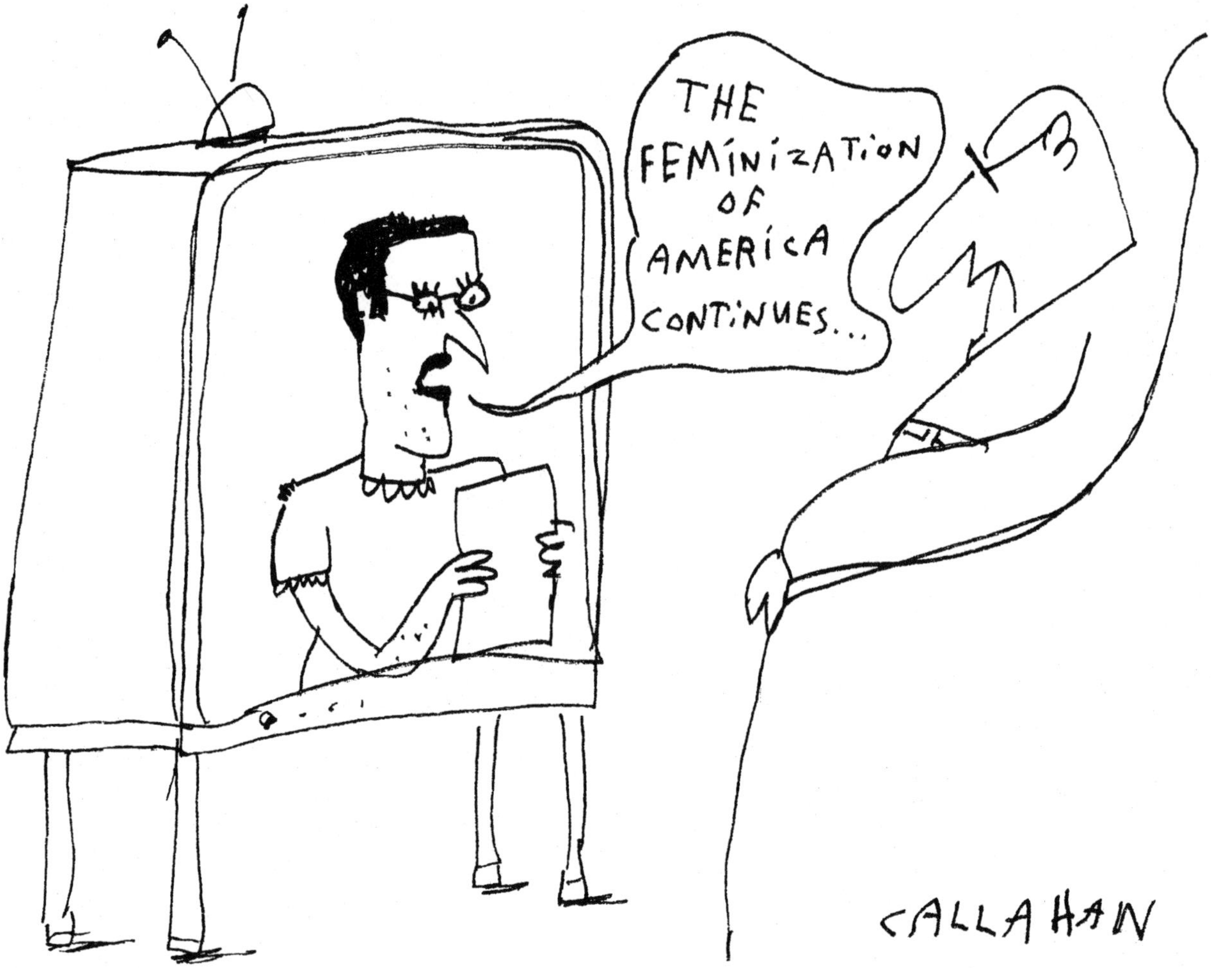
THE FEMINIZATION OF AMERICA CONTINUES...
CALLAHAN

TIME   10:02

TEMP   70°

NUMBER OF PEOPLE   9,200,389 ON MOOD ELEVATORS AT THIS MOMENT!

CALLAHAN

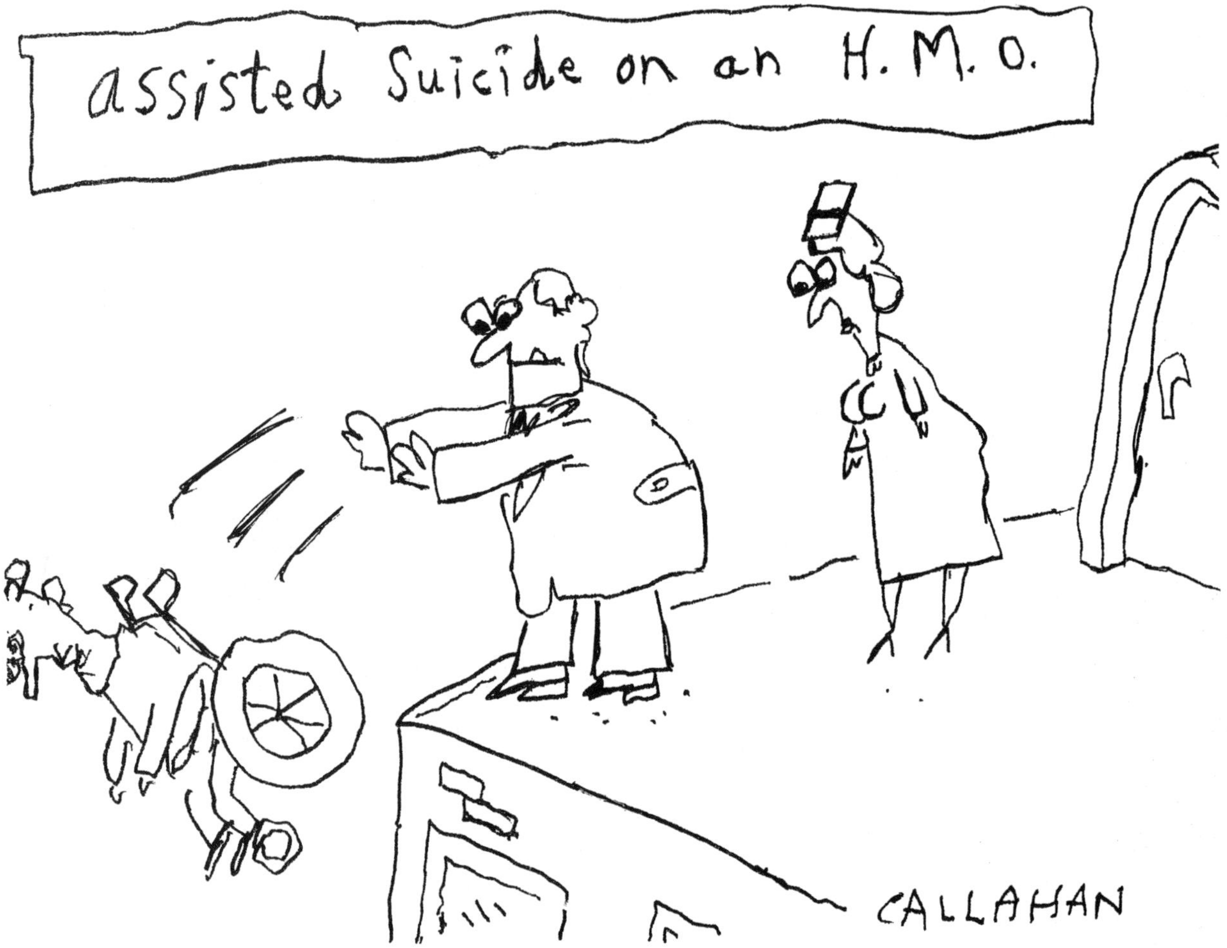
assisted Suicide on an H.M.O.
CALLAHAN

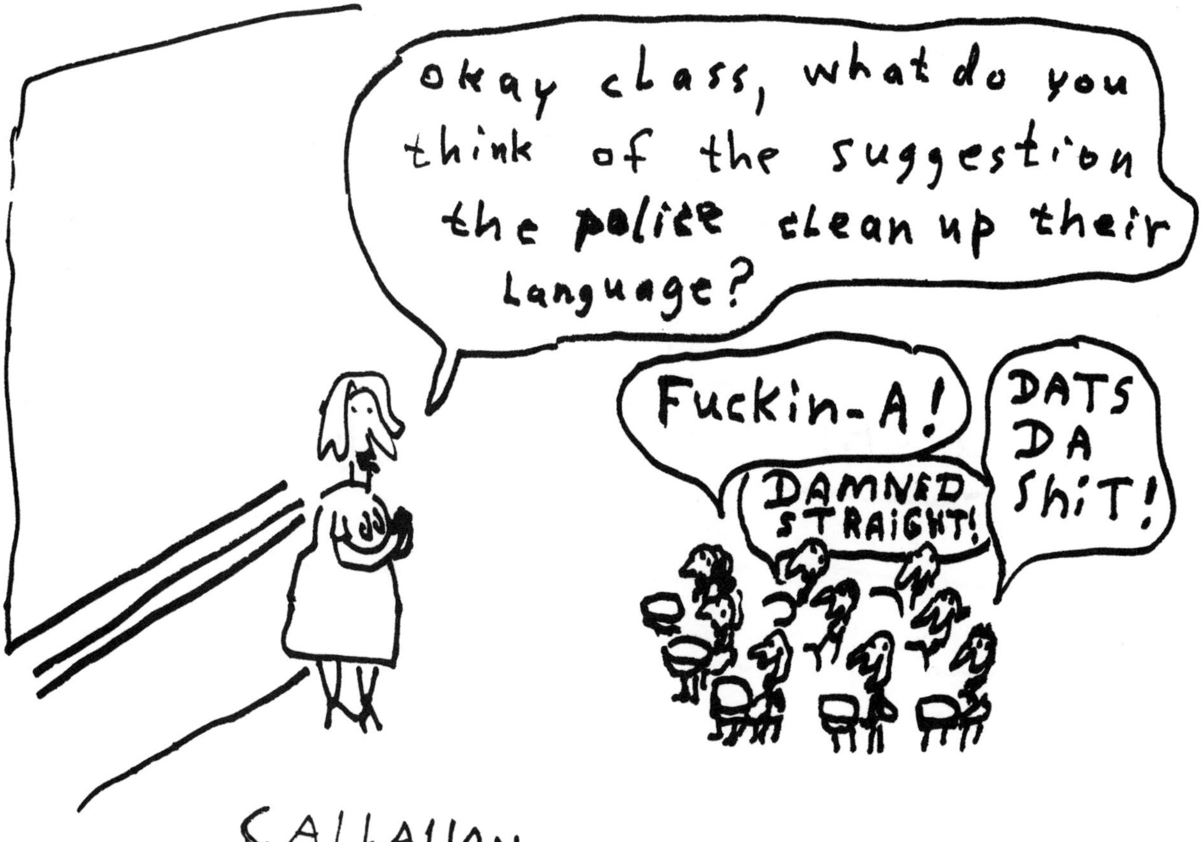
okay class, what do you think of the suggestion the police clean up their language?
Fuckin-A!
DAMNED STRAIGHT!
DATS DA SHiT!

CALLAHAN

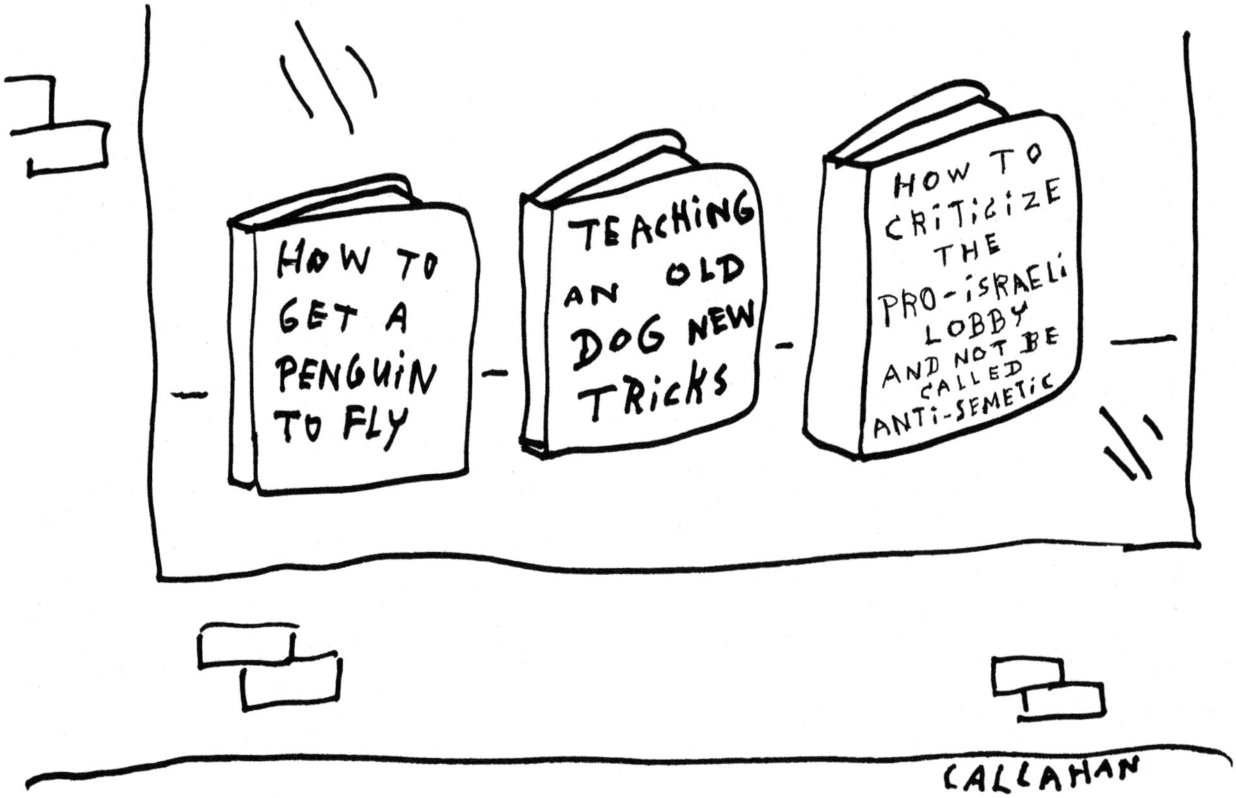
HOW TO GET A PENGUIN TO FLY
TEACHING AN OLD DOG NEW TRICKS
HOW TO CRITICIZE THE PRO-ISRAELI LOBBY AND NOT BE CALLED ANTI-SEMETIC
CALLAHAN

senator Kerry

CALLAHAN

63

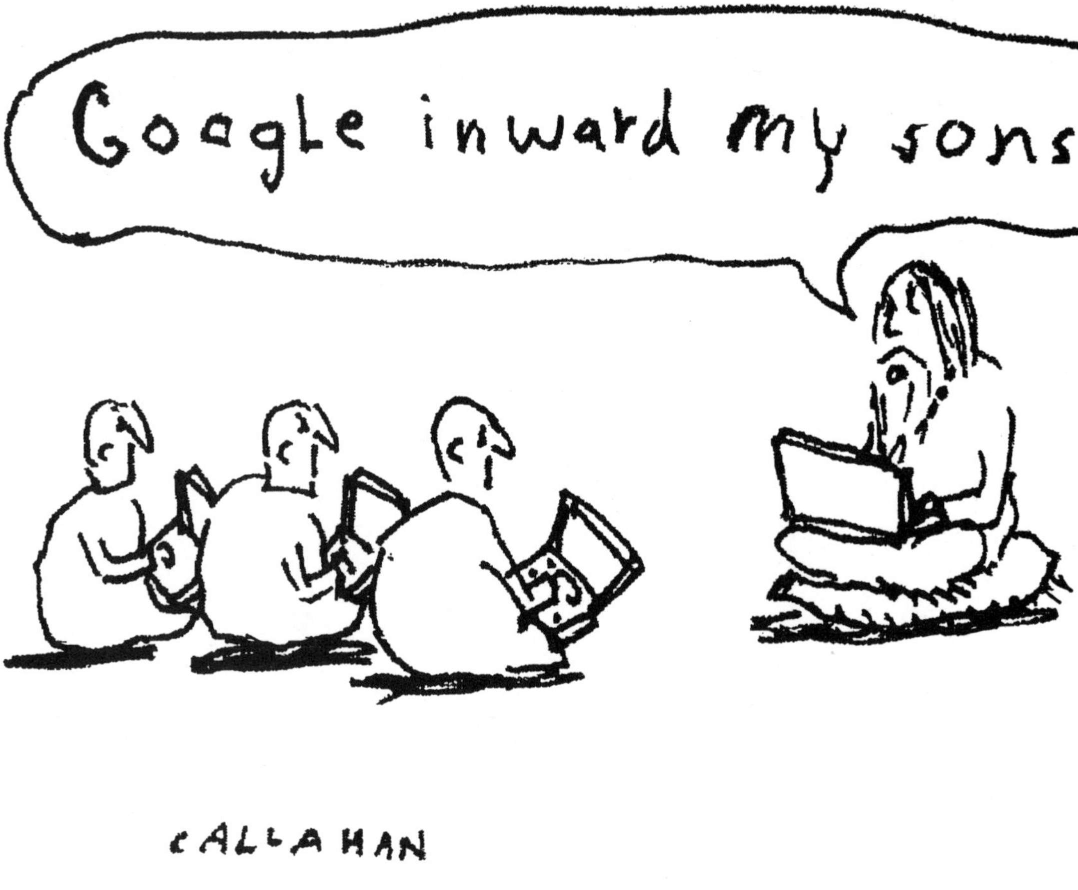
Google inward my sons...
CALLAHAN

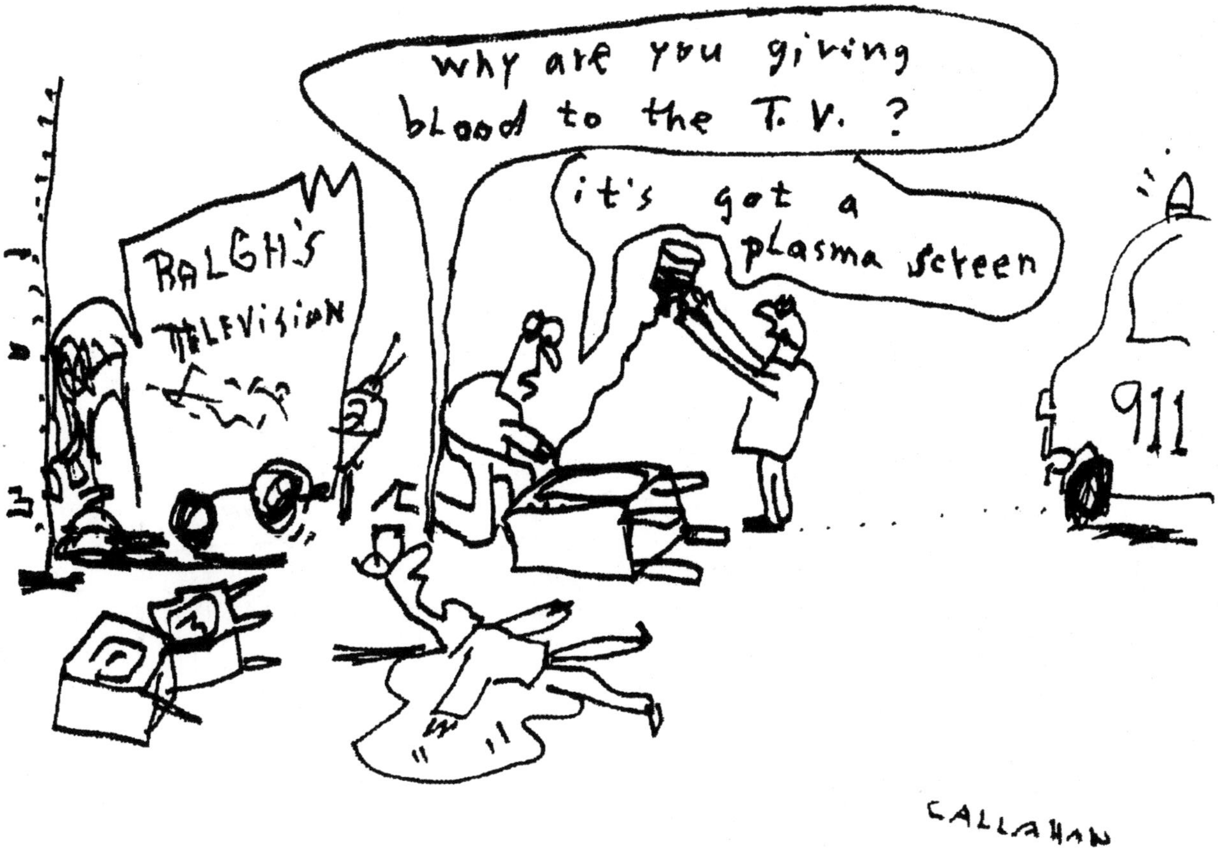

why are you giving blood to the T.V.?
it's got a plasma screen
RALGH'S TELEVISION
911
CALLAHAN

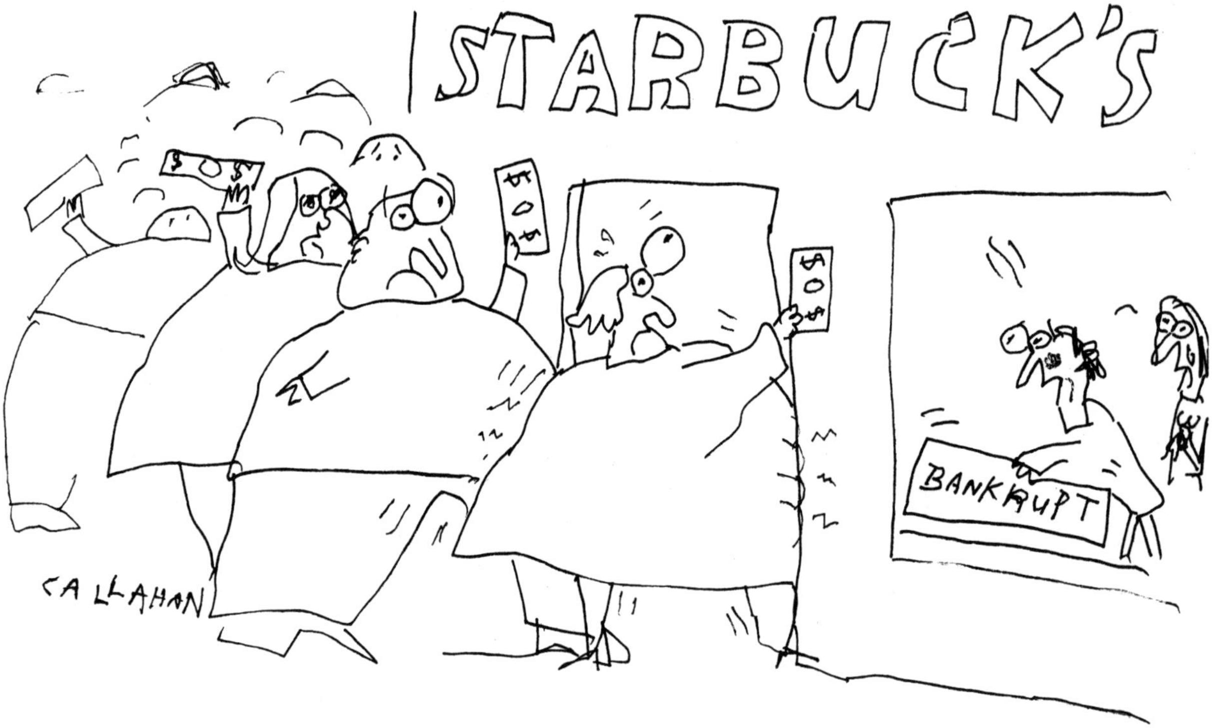
STARBUCK'S
BANKRUPT
CALLAHAN

People consume too many blended drinks and get so fat
they can't get through the door!

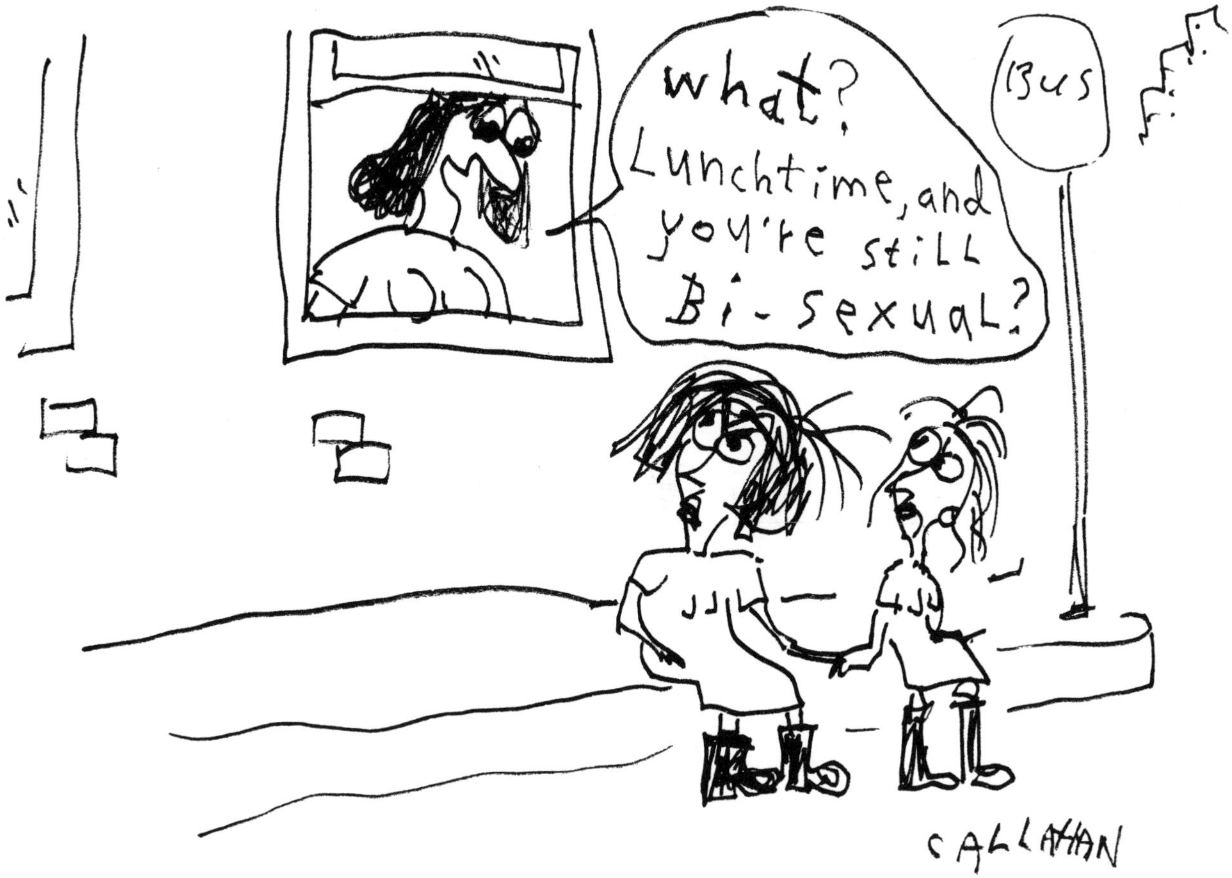
what? Lunchtime, and you're still Bi-sexual?
BUS
CALLAHAN

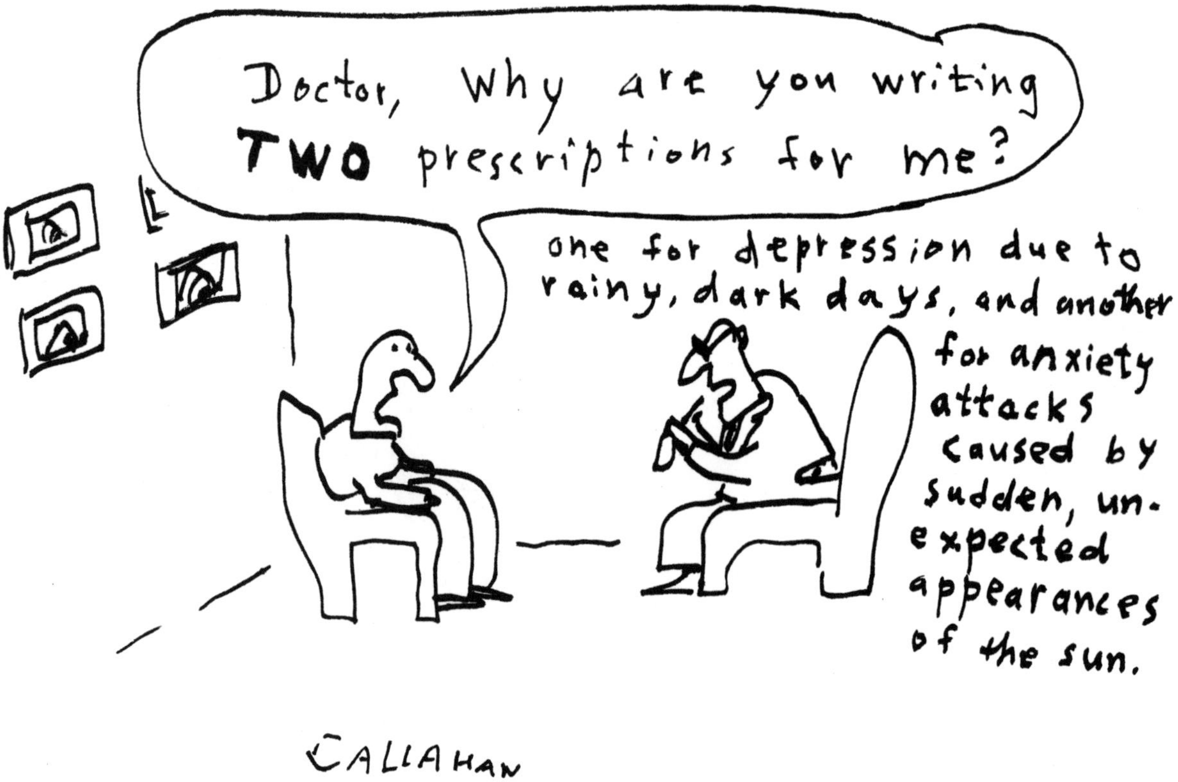
Doctor, why are you writing TWO prescriptions for me?
One for depression due to rainy, dark days, and another for anxiety attacks caused by sudden, unexpected appearances of the sun.
CALLAHAN

'Embedded' journalists   'inbredded' jouralists

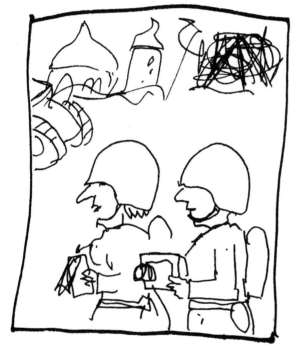

CALLAHAN

73

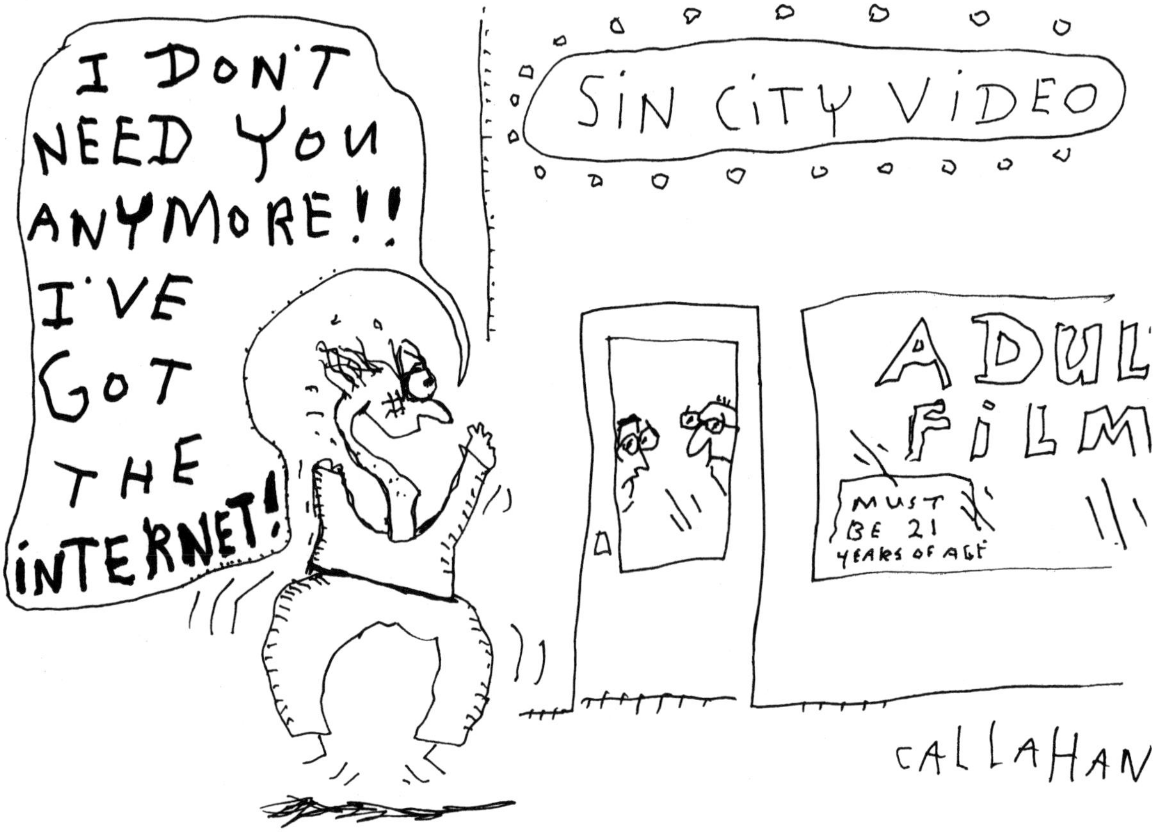
I DON'T NEED YOU ANYMORE!! I'VE GOT THE INTERNET!
SIN CITY VIDEO
ADUL
FILM
MUST BE 21 YEARS OF AGE
CALLAHAN

what are the side effects of your new medication?
headache, nausea, and diarrhea
what's the medication for?
headache nausea and diarrhea
CALLAHAN

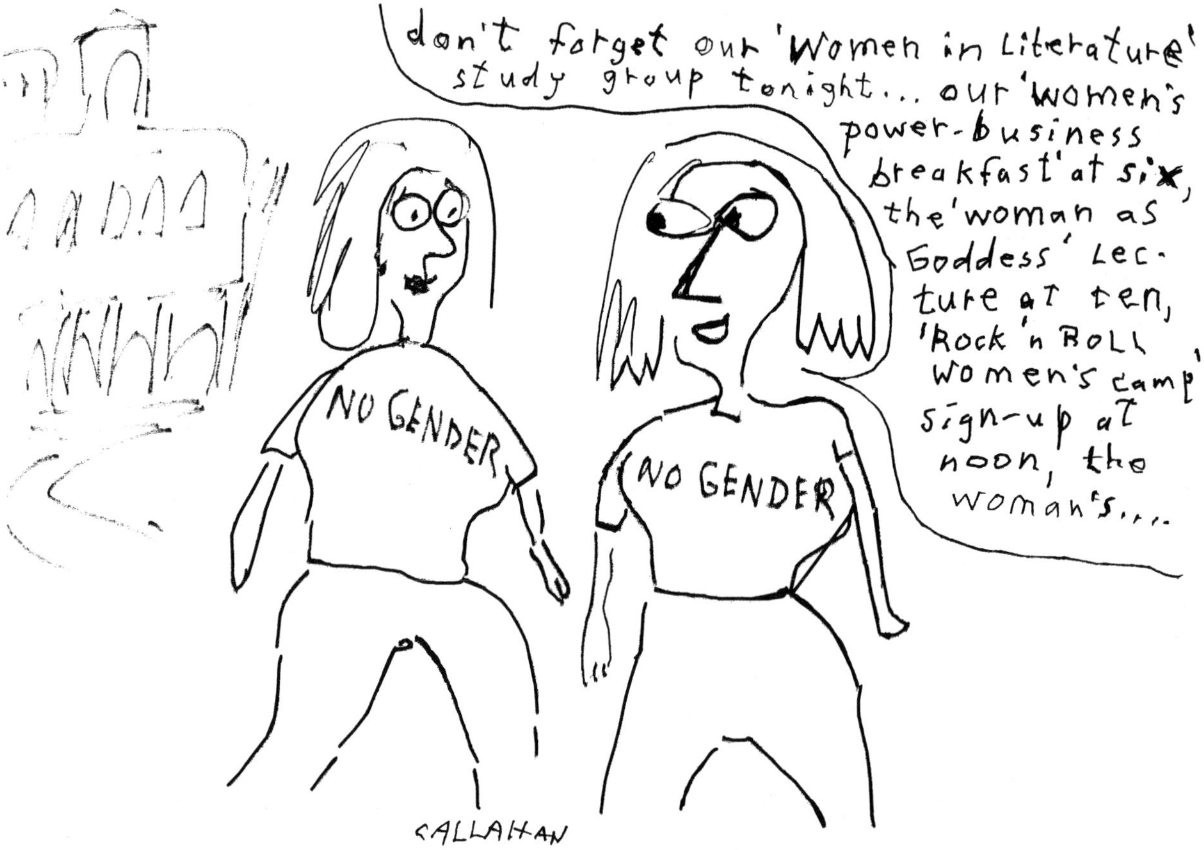
don't forget our 'Women in Literature' study group tonight... our 'Women's power-business breakfast' at six, the 'woman as Goddess' lecture at ten, 'Rock 'n Roll Women's camp' sign-up at noon, the woman's....
NO GENDER
NO GENDER
CALLAHAN

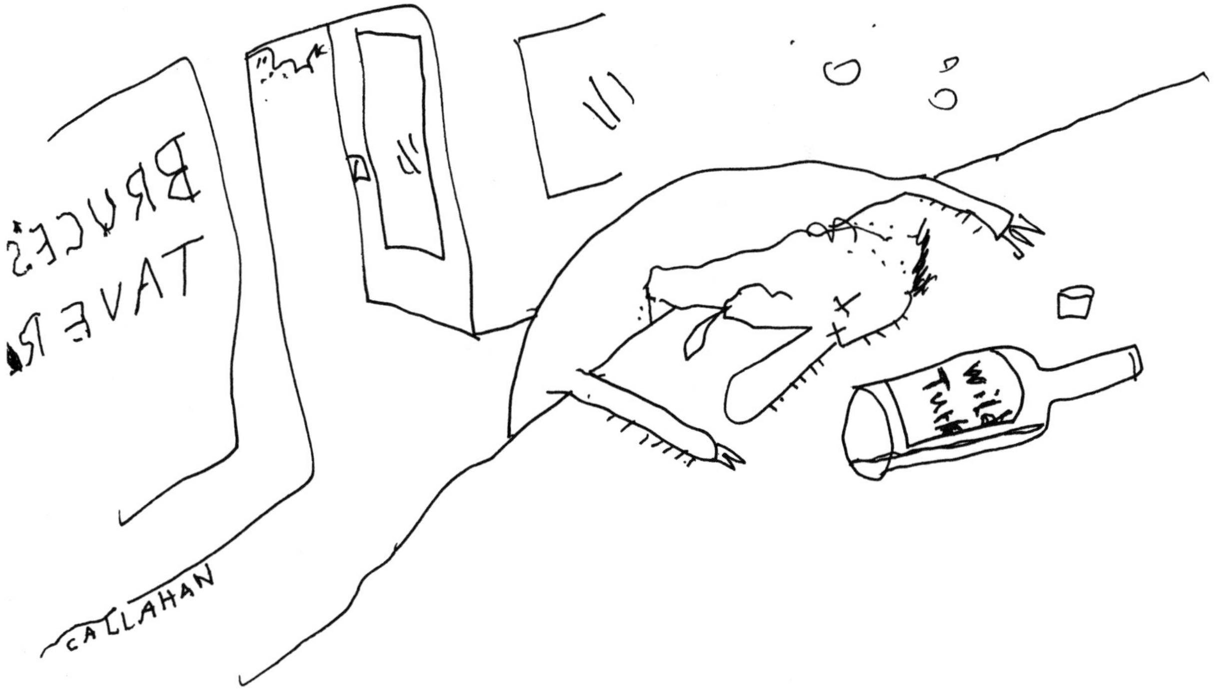
BRUCE'S
CALLAHAN

Queer eye for the straight rye.

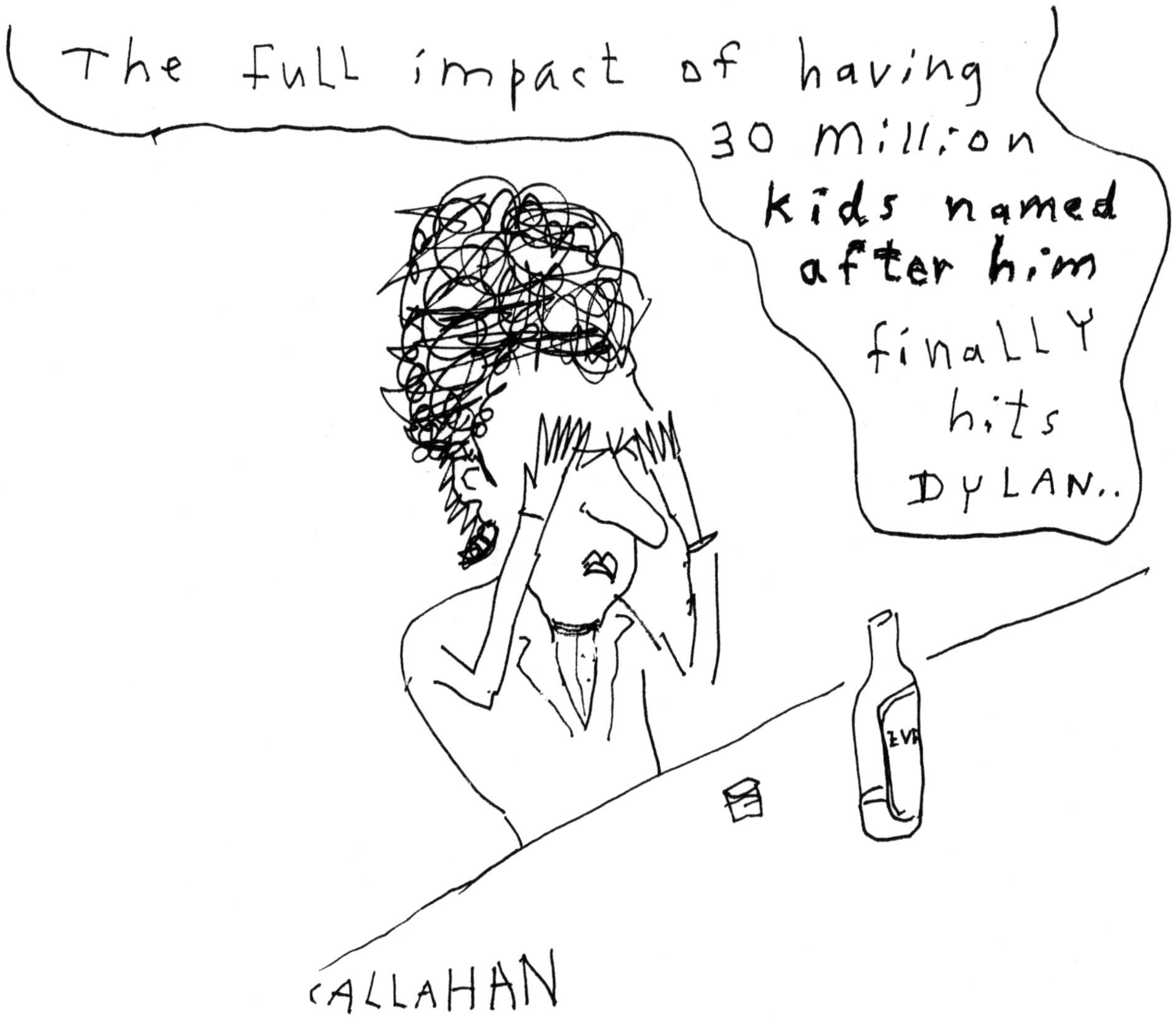
The full impact of having 30 million kids named after him finally hits DYLAN..
CALLAHAN

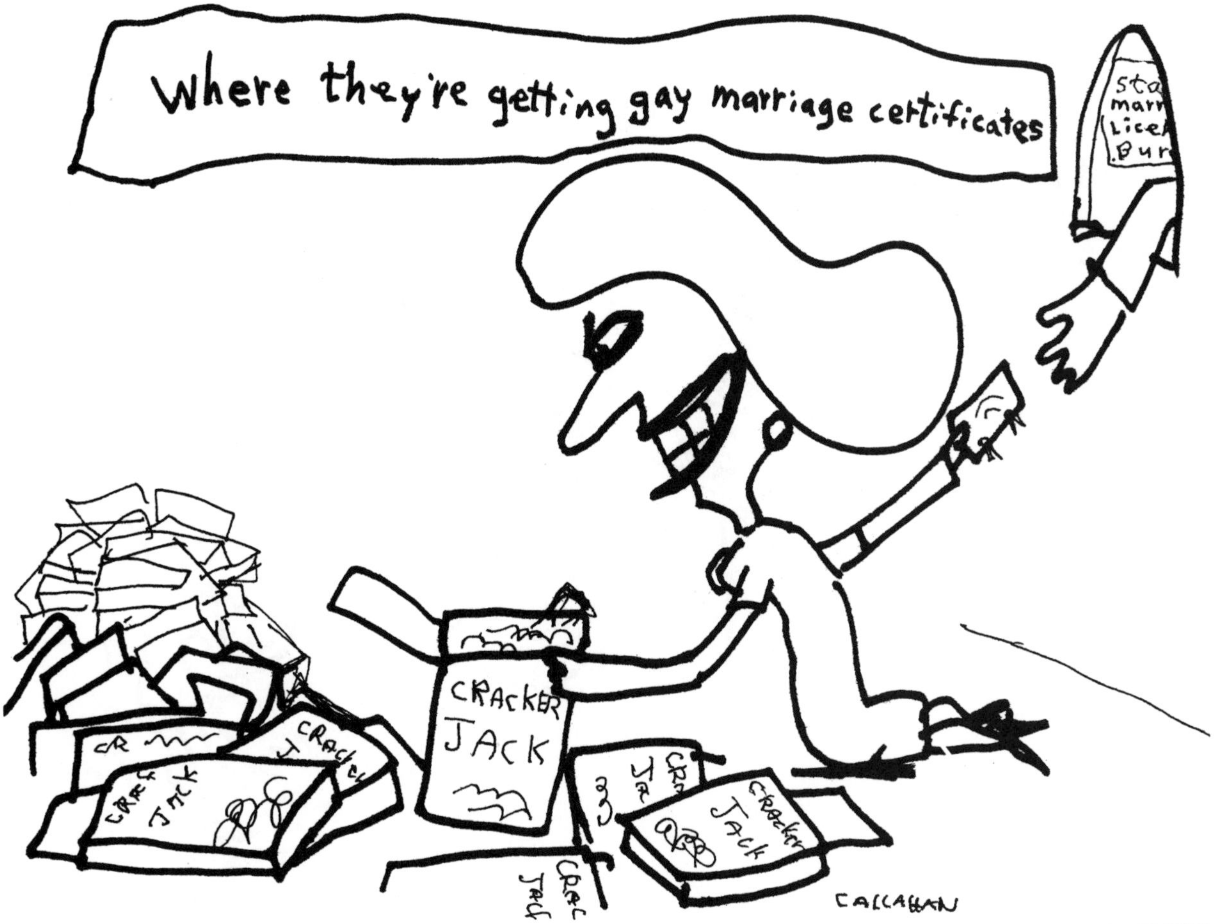
Where they're getting gay marriage certificates
CRACKER JACK
CALLAHAN

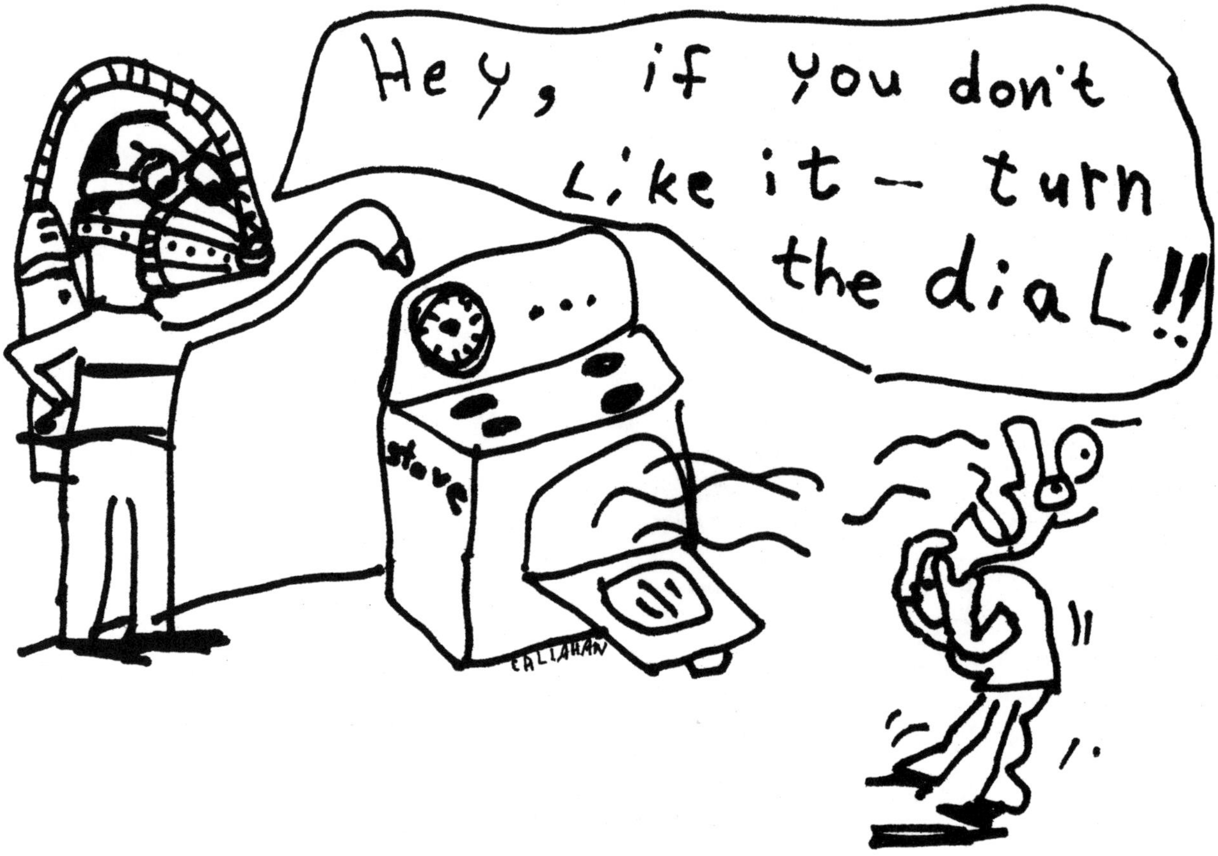
Hey, if you don't like it – turn the diaL!!
stove
CALLAHAN

A radio shock jock at home after work...

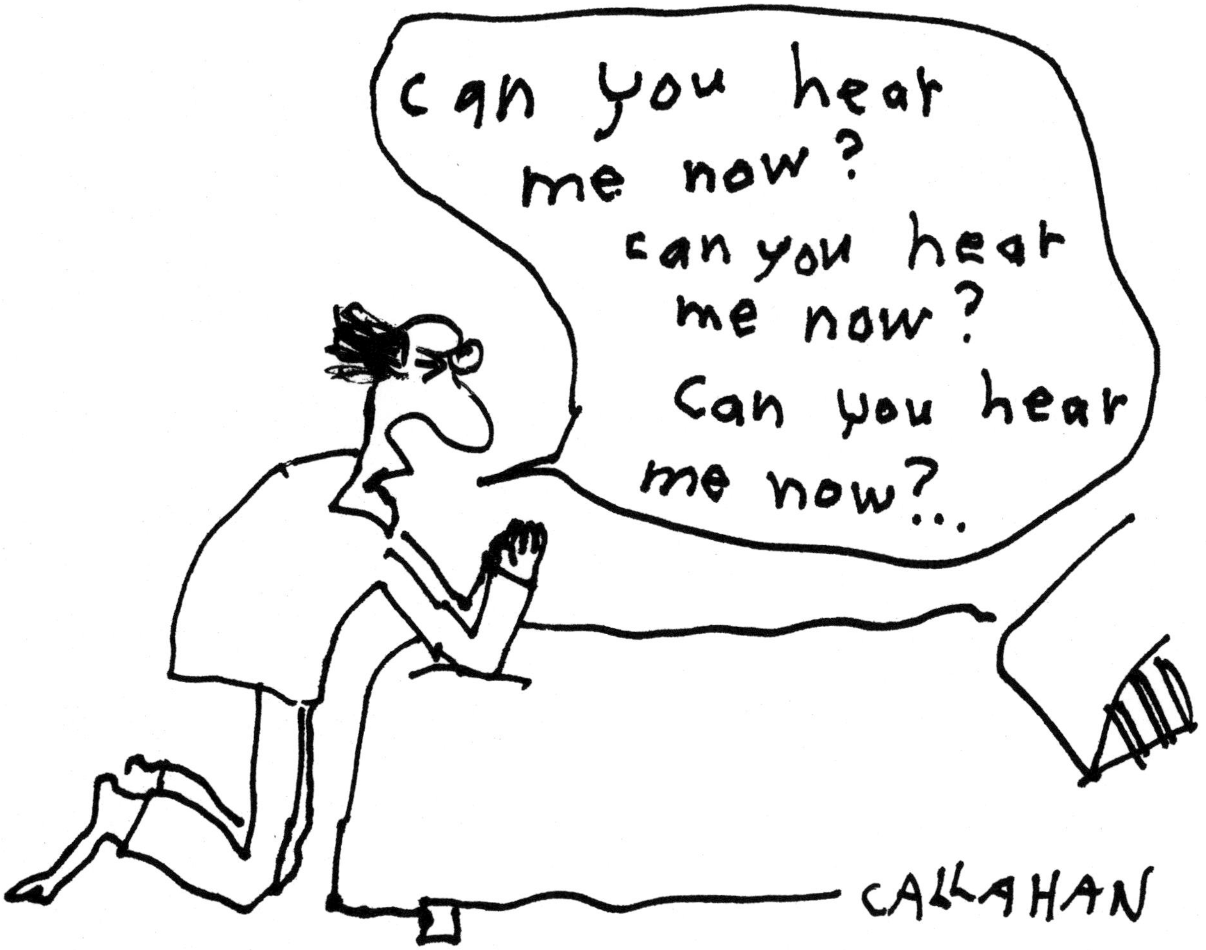
can you hear me now? can you hear me now? Can you hear me now?...
CALLAHAN

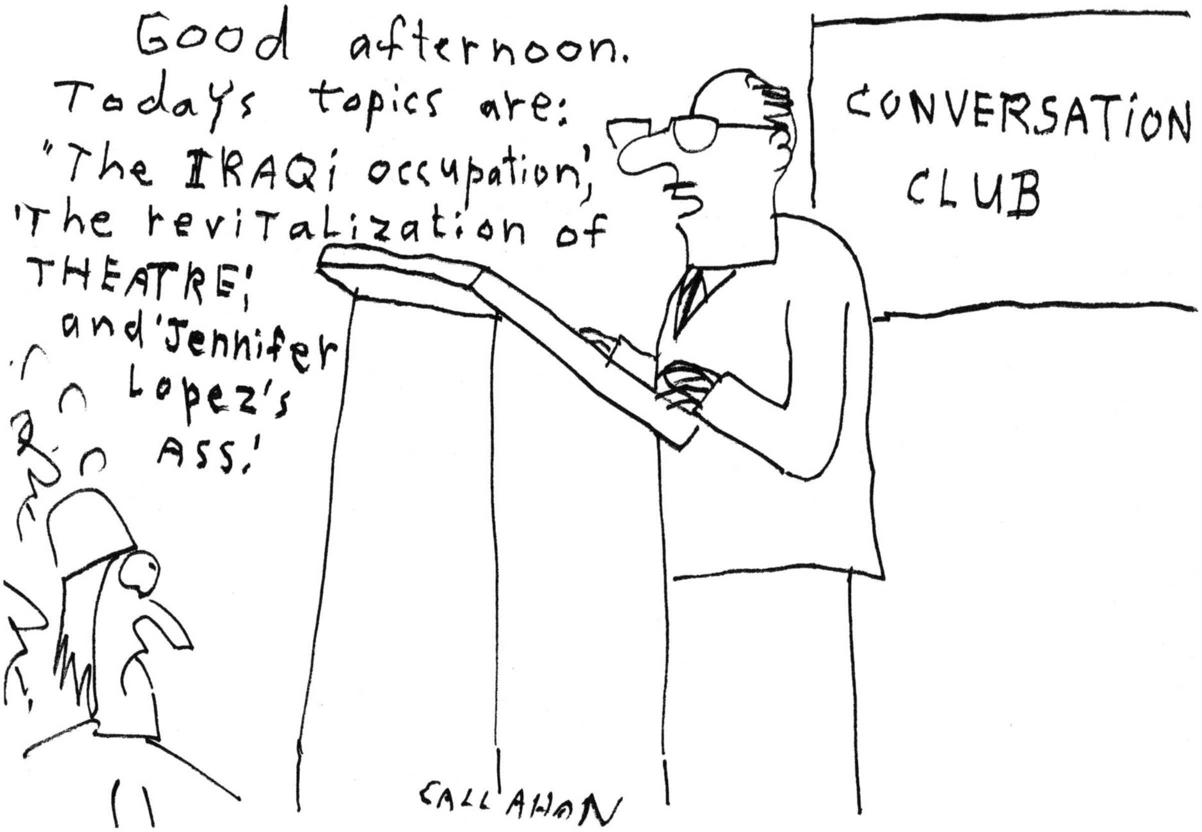
Good afternoon. Todays topics are: "The IRAQi occupation,' 'The revitalization of THEATRE,' and 'Jennifer Lopez's ASS.'
CONVERSATION CLUB
CALLAHAN

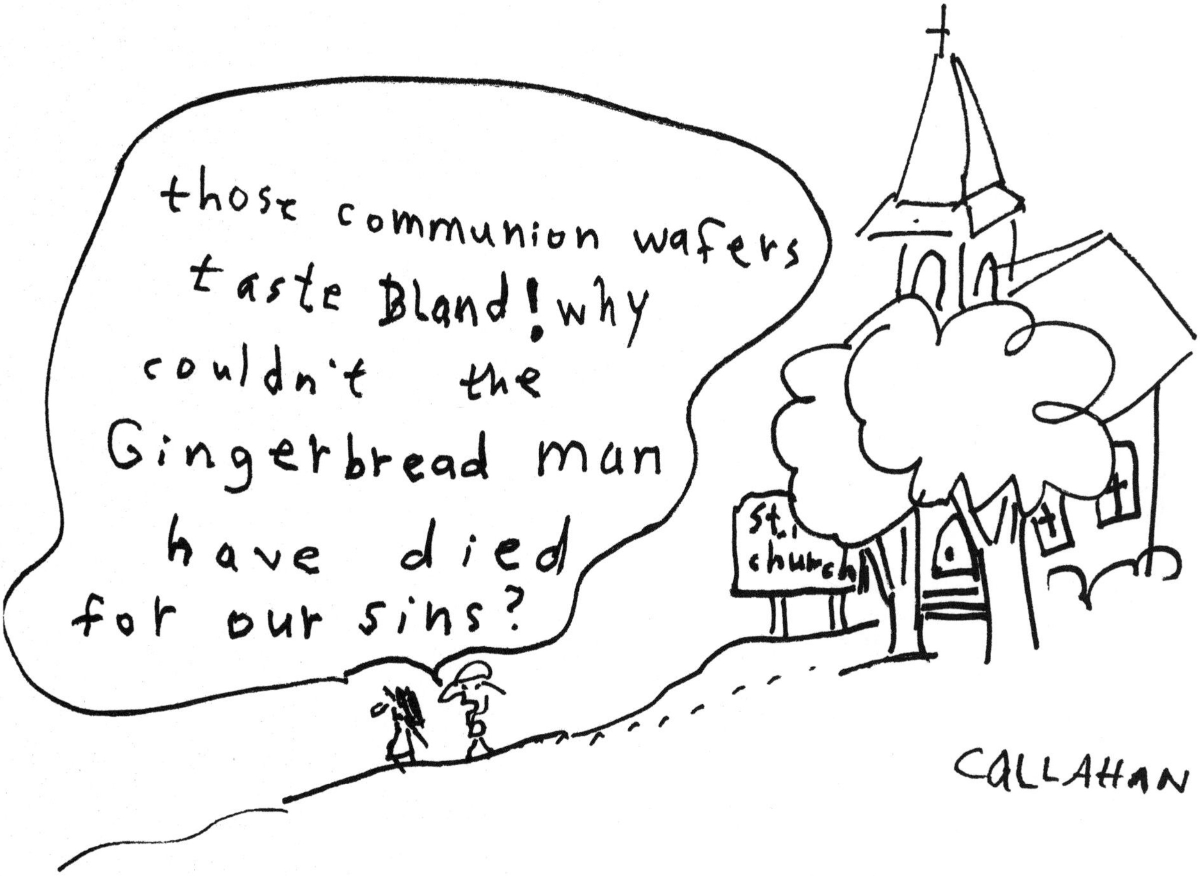
those communion wafers taste Bland! why couldn't the Gingerbread man have died for our sins?
St.
church
CALLAHAN

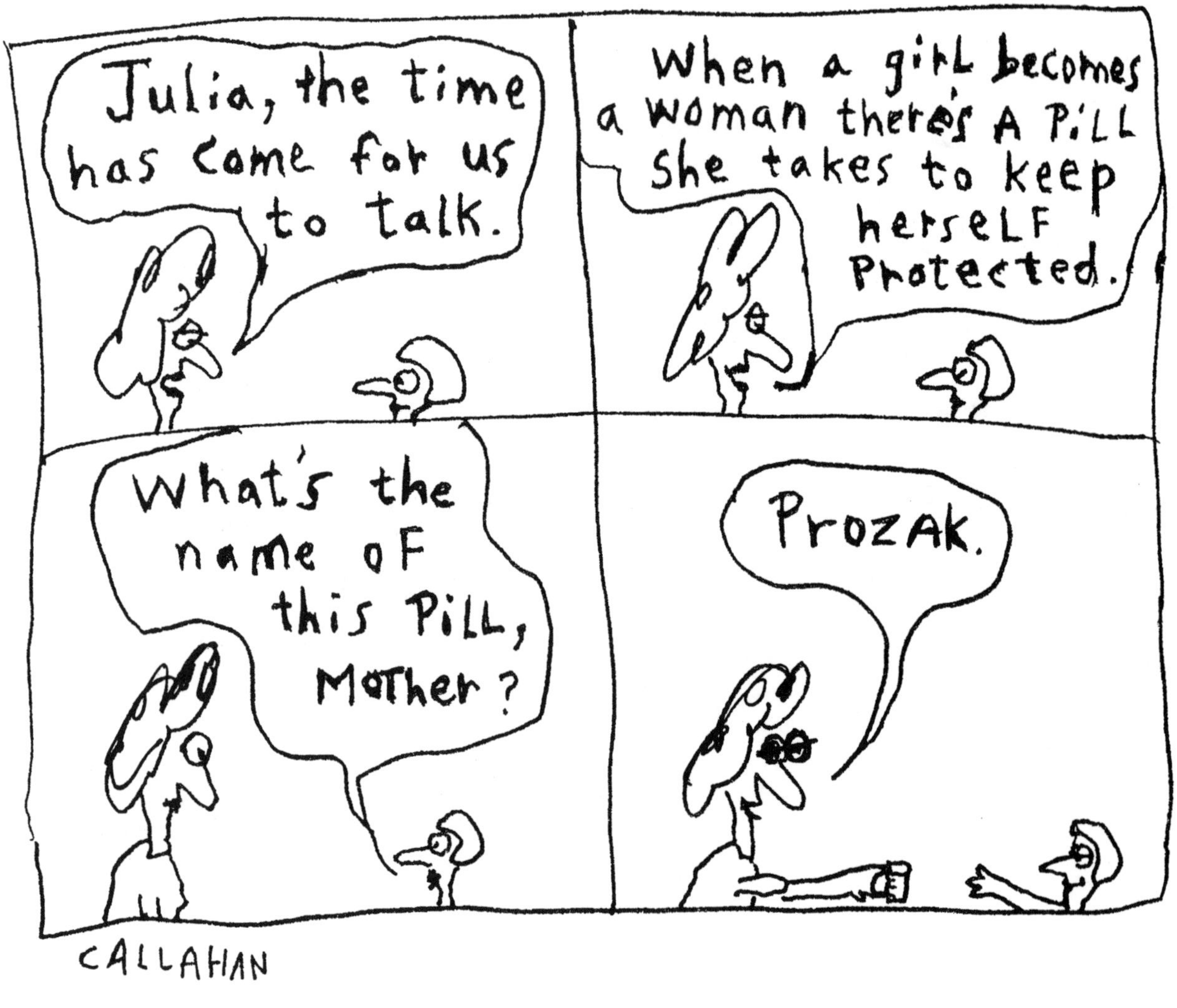
Julia, the time has come for us to talk.
When a girl becomes a woman there's A PiLL She takes to keep herseLF Protected.
What's the name oF this PiLL, Mother?
ProzAK.
CALLAHAN

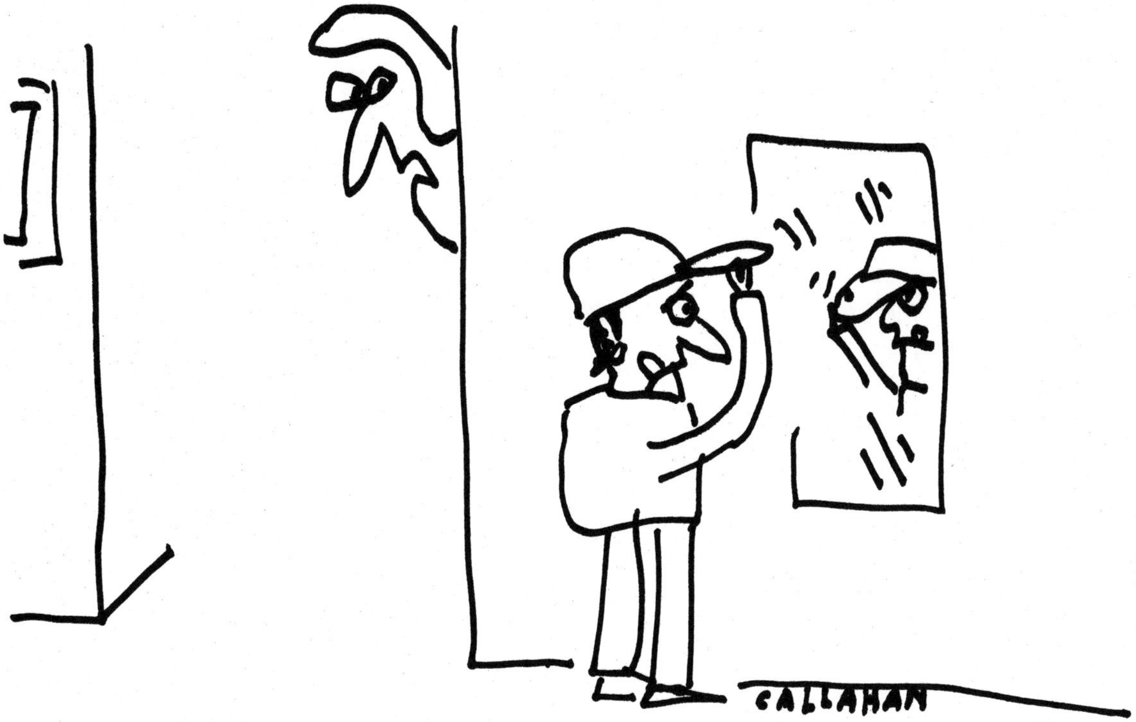
CALLAHAN

"Your hat is properly crooked, now get to school!"

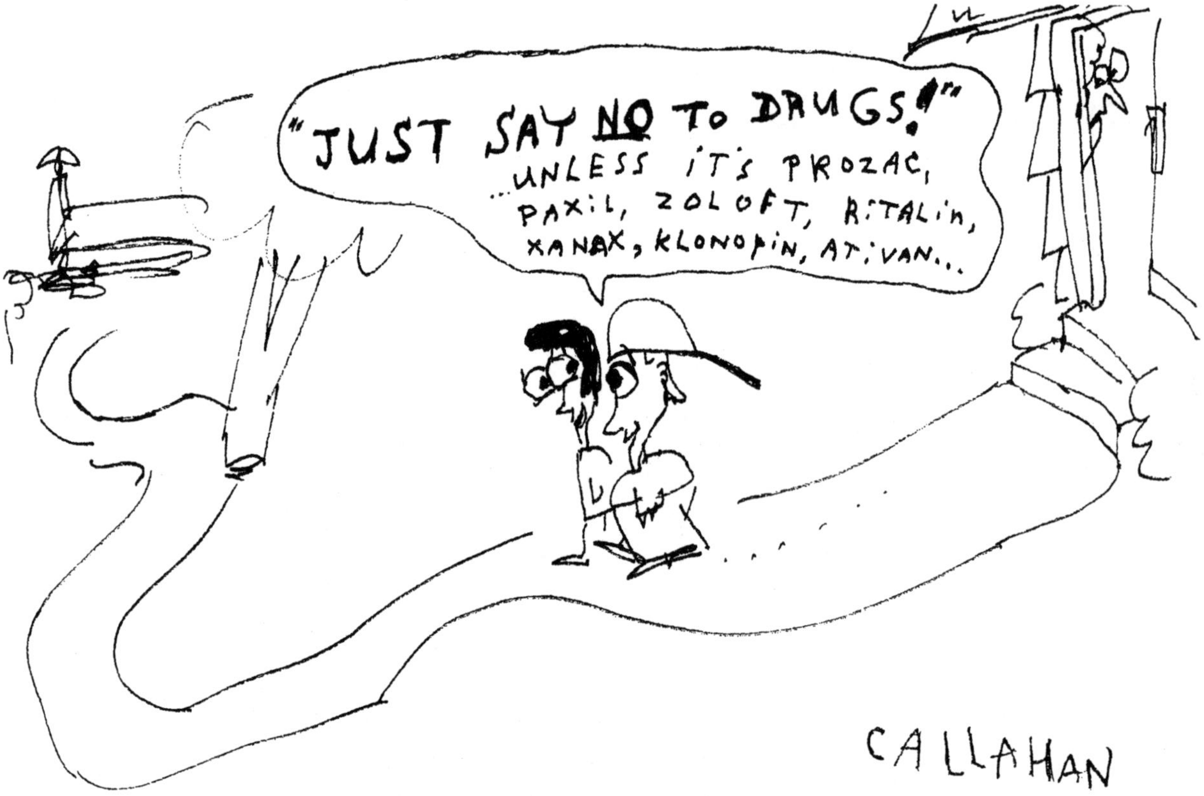
"JUST SAY NO TO DRUGS!" ...UNLESS IT'S PROZAC, PAXIL, ZOLOFT, RITALIN, XANAX, KLONOPIN, ATIVAN...
CALLAHAN

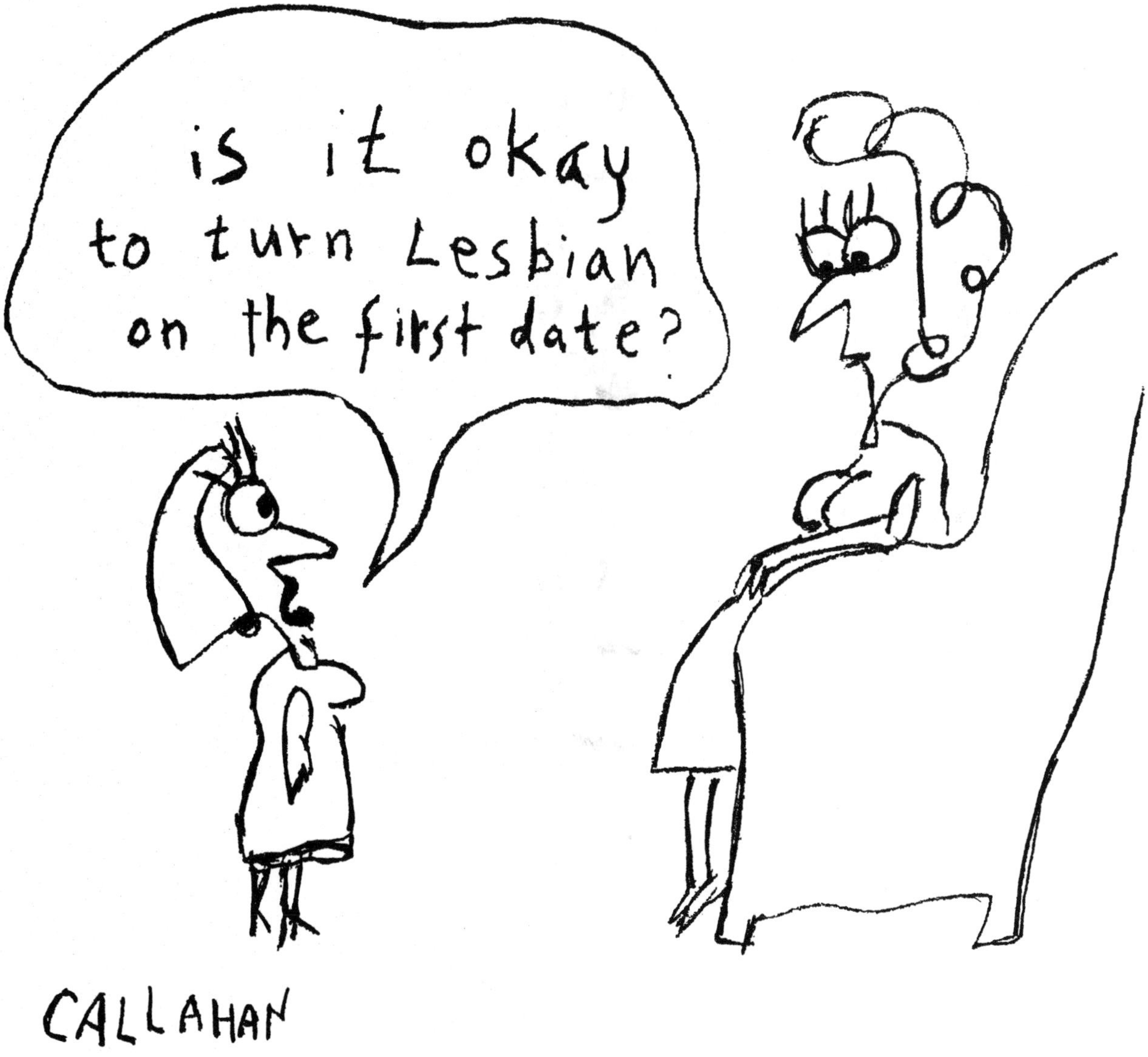
is it okay to turn Lesbian on the first date?
CALLAHAN

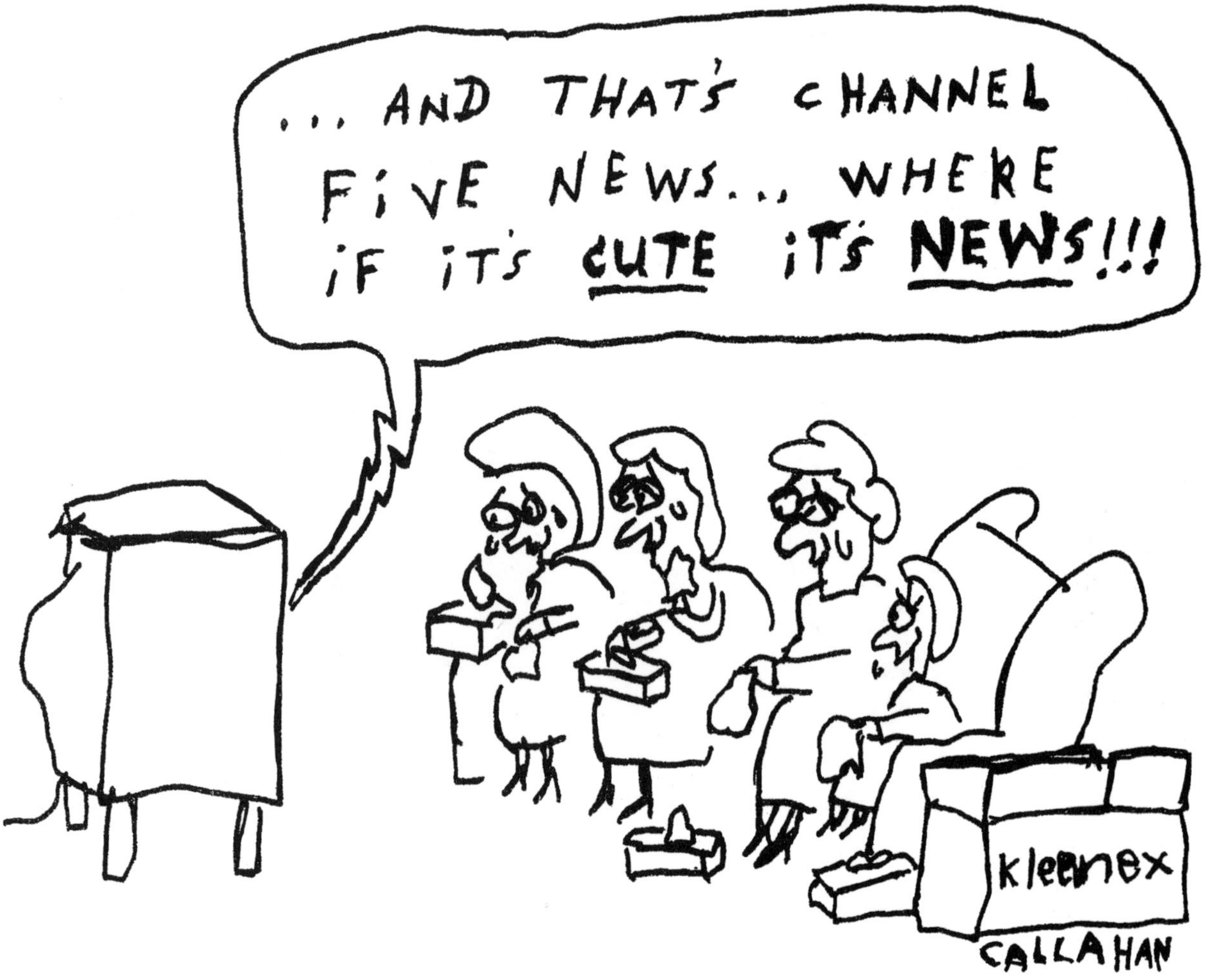
...AND THAT'S CHANNEL FIVE NEWS... WHERE IF IT'S CUTE IT'S NEWS!!!
kleenex
CALLAHAN

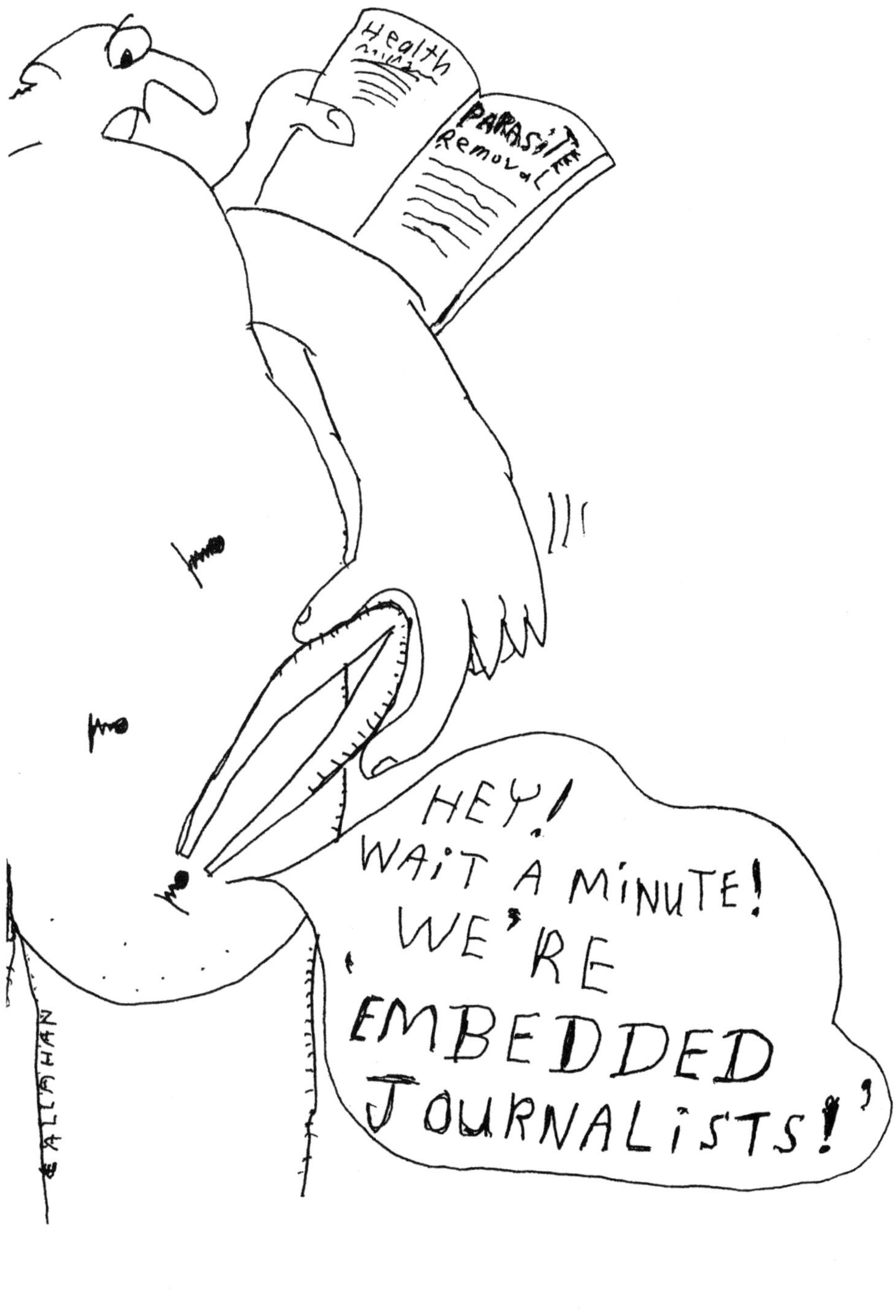
Health
PARASITE Removal
HEY! WAIT A MINUTE! 'WE'RE EMBEDDED JOURNALISTS!'
CALLAHAN

LOOK... IT'S MICHAEL MOORE, WITH HIS LATEST BOOK, 'STUPID WHITE MEN!'
..QUICK, THINK OF SOMETHING TO SAY!
...UH, MISTER MOORE... I SEE YOU'VE WRITTEN AN AUTO-BIOGRAPHY!
stupid white man
CALLAHAN

Interview with John Callahan

Ballantine Books: Words like "twisted" and "sick" are often applied to your cartoons by fans and detractors alike. Is that a response you set out to achieve, or does it just happen to work out that way?

John Callahan: I kind of have to be reminded that my humor is what people call sick or twisted, because it's all just normal thinking for me. It's the way I see life.

BB: Do you think you would have become a cartoonist if not for the 1972 accident that left you a quadriplegic?

JC: I probably would have, because I'd been doing it as a kid. There was a long time in my life where I was waiting for my drawing ability to catch up to my sense of humor. Some might say it still hasn't!

BB: What led you to take up cartooning again after the accident?

JC: It was when I was in college, at the age of about thirty-one. It was 1982. I'd been sober for a couple of years by then, and my creative juices were starting to flow again. I felt that I wanted to express myself after years of drunkenness.

BB: Did the accident lead you to rely more heavily on drinking for a period of time, or were you already headed in the direction of alcoholism?

JC: I was a passenger in a car that was wrecked. It was my own car, and I was letting someone else drive. He was drunk, but then so was I. So even though I wasn't driving, a lot of what happened was basically my fault. Yeah, I think that the disability caused the drinking to increase. There's such a vulturous boredom—that's a phrase from a Sylvia Plath poem called "The Hanging Man"—a high level of stress and boredom around being paralyzed. Wanting relief from that made me increase my drinking quite a bit.

BB: Did your experience of the accident and life as a quadriplegic lend your sense of humor its dark and ironic edge, or were those qualities always there? And do they help you to survive mentally?

JC: Those qualities were always there. I had some strange knocks as a child, some traumatic experiences as a very little kid, and I think that's what twisted me in this fashion. But the wheelchair didn't exactly help . . . or hurt, I guess I should say.

BB: Were those characteristics or qualities of mind, which come out so strongly in your cartoons, helpful in coming to terms with your paralysis?

JC: I've used humor as a buffer and a kind of lubricant for myself to help me sort of skid my way along tough spots many times in my life, and I think it's the humor that's allowed me to reduce the trauma of things and put them into perspective. It's just a natural response for me. I think it's amusing when people think that you gain a sense of humor through some trauma. It's inborn.

BB: It sounds as if cartooning serves the same kind of purpose for you as drinking did.

JC: Yeah, it really does. They're both vehicles, you know? A vehicle can be neurotic in nature but still serve a purpose. I mean, any neurosis serves a purpose, but it's a double-edged sword. It can eventually become so self-defeating that you must release it. That's what happened finally with my drinking.

BB: How long did it take you to start selling your cartoons?

JC: I began selling them very quickly, because I was given very rapid encouragement from *Penthouse* magazine and from different papers in Portland where I was working. This was back in 1982 or 1983.

BB: Does being a person with disabilities give you permission to attack subjects that other cartoonists might shy away from?

JC: It seems to have worked out that way. There's a sort of feeling that people get. They think they can't attack me because I've suffered so much or something, and that makes me all the more determined to provoke them. It's a strange sort of license that they give me. I've always felt that I have a license to kill. It's a helpful feeling for a cartoonist.

BB: Do you feel an obligation to focus on subjects that society views through a lens of pity or compassion, or prefers not to look at at all?

JC: No, I'm attracted to my subjects because they're such hot-button issues for me. I was just born with this perverse sense of "Don't tell me I can't attack that subject." The more you tell me I can't attack some subject, the more likely I'll do just that, especially when the people telling me what I can't or shouldn't do are groups that have very little of a sense of humor about themselves or anything else, like feminists or the whole politically correct movement. I mean, I live in Portland, right? It's got this weirdly predominant feminist energy. People actually comment on the mean women that live here. It makes me react. I can't help it.

BB: Have you ever thought of living somewhere else?

JC: I'm drawn to Philadelphia, even though it's a dirty, horrible place. I've only been there on book tours. I don't know the town very well. I'd like to stay there for a couple of weeks and get to know it better.

BB: The City of Brotherly Love.

JC: Maybe in a perverse sort of way . . .

BB: What kind of relationship do you have with the disabilities-rights community?

JC: I don't have one. I'm very often called by them and asked to be active in what they're doing, but I feel more comfortable just doing my own part somewhere off in the distance.

BB: Who are some of the cartoonists or other artists and writers that have influenced you most?

JC: My biggest influences have been poets and songwriters. I mentioned Sylvia Plath earlier. Dylan Thomas. Bob Dylan. John Prine, who actually became a friend of mine. I admire them because of the way they're able to transmit truth. That's something I try to do in my own humble way. It's why I don't do standard daily-paper types of cartoons with, you know, the boss chasing the secretary around the desk.

BB: Do cartoon ideas come to you out of the blue, or have you worked to develop a way of generating new ideas for cartoons?

JC: When I was younger, I did develop a method for generating cartoons, and I worked hard to learn the gimmicks, the tricks and tools of the trade. As the years went by, it all became second nature to me. Now I'm set up like a Venus Flytrap, and when something comes close, I snap at it, and suddenly it's done. It's effortless, and at this point it's almost unconscious.

BB: What do you mean by gimmicks?

JC: You may have a great sense of humor, and you may have the drawing ability, but to make it as a cartoonist you've got to learn how to combine them and to construct the various elements out of which jokes are conveyed in this medium. There are conventions, like the old tin-cup joke or the blind-man-with-a-sign routine. You start out with those kinds of things, and then you grow beyond them, into your own voice, your own style.

BB: What materials do you use in your work? Have you experimented with any of the computer drawing software that's out there now?

JC: I've never used a computer to draw. I draw on $8\frac{1}{2}$ x 11 bond paper with a Sharpie. Very simple.

BB: Do you listen to music while you do your cartooning?

JC: I write music a lot. I'm a songwriter. There's music in my head constantly. I have thousands of lyrics always coming and going in my head. I listen to music twenty-four hours a day. I listen to everything from the Yeah Yeah Yeahs to Beethoven, everything from The Strokes to Pete Seeger.

BB: Are you going to record and release any of your own songs?

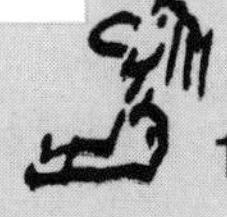

JC: I have a homemade CD collection of songs that I wrote. Certain famous rock-and-roll stars have offered to show it to their labels, and I may take advantage of that. So I'm working on getting my songs out there. Originally, I was just trying to get people to sing my songs, but now it seems that some people like my voice a lot and think I should do the singing myself.

BB: I haven't heard you sing, but your voice has a kind of Tom Waits quality to it.

JC: No, today I just have a rough voice from talking too much yesterday. My normal singing voice has a strange sweetness and purity to it that some people like. I don't much care for it myself. I'd rather have a voice like Tom Waits. He's kind of my mentor.

BB: As a songwriter?

JC: Yeah, he likes my songwriting. In fact, he once sang one of my songs onto my answering machine.

BB: Tell us about your new collection, *Levels of Insanity*.

JC: Well, there's a very up-to-date feeling about this collection. It deals with the increasing craziness of the culture, the increasing tension and stress and nuttiness. It touches on the presidential election and all the hot-button issues of the campaign, although I wouldn't call the cartoons political in any kind of traditional sense.

BB: Is the post-9/11 world a difficult one for cartoonists?

JC: It used to be. Comedians and cartoonists had to back off of certain subjects for a while. But I think people have gotten their humor back. I was on the Dave Attell show, you know, *Insomniac*, on Comedy Central, and it was a very irreverent show, the topics we were dealing with, and how hard-core my humor was, but they keep replaying it, and I get a lot of good feedback from people who have seen it. To me, that's a sign that everybody is back to their usual sick old selves.

BB: What about the war on terror and the fighting in Afghanistan and Iraq? What effect has that had?

JC: The political cartoonists are dealing with it every day, of course. For me, I've gone out of my way to ridicule Bush, specifically about this forced war that he's created. I'm not usually that political about such things, but since 9/11 my perspective about America and its place in the world has changed, partly as a result of what the Republicans have done in the aftermath. The manipulations of Bush in particular have driven me way back to . . . Well, look. I've been very sympathetic to the conservatives over the past few years. Almost as a way of irritating the left, who are so politically correct. But now, because of things like the Patriot Act, the lies about Iraq, and the blindness of people to the power of the pro-Israeli lobby to drive our country, I find myself being slapped into a sobriety that I haven't felt since I was in my early twenties.

BB: I know that Robin Williams bought the rights to your bestselling autobiography, *Don't Worry, He Won't Get Far on Foot*. Is there any news on that front?

JC: I've become friends with Robin Williams, and that's been fun, but there are so many variables that have to fall into place. Right now there's no way to say how long it might be before he moves ahead with the movie, or even if it will ever get made at all. Of course, the book has stayed in print all these years, so there is definitely an audience out there. I don't have good legs myself, but the autobiography does.

BB: What other projects are you working on now?

JC: I've been trying to get something going with a show on cable TV, but I can't really mention anything about it. I don't want to jinx it.

BB: Do you laugh at your own cartoons?

JC: I have an extremely crude cartoon that's coming out in today's paper, the local weekly. I can't wait to see it. It's a picture of a proctologist probing a patient on the table in his office, and he's saying, "You're not going to believe this, Mr. Smith...but they've opened a new Starbucks up your ass!" I laughed when I drew that one, and I'm going to laugh again when I see it in the paper.

BB: I just read that Starbucks is expanding, in fact.

JC: Jesus. Soon they'll be running it through the spigots in your house.